Ending Mozambique's War

CAMERON HUME

ENDING MOZAMBIQUE'S WAR

The Role of Mediation and Good Offices

UNITED STATES INSTITUTE OF PEACE PRESS
Washington, D.C.

The views expressed in this book are those of the author alone. They do not necessarily reflect views of the United States Institute of Peace.

United States Institute of Peace
1550 M Street, N.W.
Washington, D.C. 20005-1708

First published 1994

Printed in the United States of America

The paper used in this publication meets the minimum requirements of American National Standard for Information Sciences—Permanence of Paper for Printed Library Materials, ANSI Z39.48-1984.

Library of Congress Cataloging-in-Publication Data
Hume, Cameron R., 1947–
A path to peace : ending Mozambique's civil war / Cameron R. Hume.
p. cm.
Includes bibliographical references and index.
ISBN 1-878379-38-0 : alk. paper. — ISBN 1-878379-37-2 (pbk.) : alk. paper
1. Mozambique—Politics and government—1975– 2. RENAMO (Organization). 3. FRELIMO. I. Title.
DT3398.H86 1994
967.905—dc20 94-28464
CIP

With thanks to Margaret, Rigmor, Laura, Heather, Jasmin, and Ivy—
For your love and understanding

Contents

Foreword ***by Chester A. Crocker*** **ix**

Preface **xiii**

1. Seeds of Conflict **3**

An Inauspicious Beginning 4
FRELIMO 8
RENAMO 13
The Community of Sant'Egidio 15
Outsiders 19

2. Starting a Dialogue **25**

Moving toward Talks: 1989 to June 1990 26
Round One: July 8–10, 1990 32
Round Two: August 11–14, 1990 35
Round Three: November 9 to December 1, 1990 41
Round Three Continued: December 19–21, 1990 47

3. Ordering the Peace Process **51**

Round Four: January 29–31, 1991 52
Maneuvering: February to April 1991 56
Round Five: May 6 to June 7, 1991 59
Round Six: August 1–7, 1991 64
Round Seven: October 1–18, 1991 68

4. Helping Negotiations Along 73

Round Eight on Political Party Law: October 21 to November 13, 1991 74
Round Nine on Election Law: December 17–20, 1991 80
Round Nine Resumed: January 20 to February 15, 1992 84
Round Nine Concluded: February 12 to March 12, 1992 90

5. Expanding the Framework 95

Preparing the Next Phase: March 15 to June 9, 1992 96
Round Ten Starts: June 10 to July 1, 1992 102
Humanitarian Assistance: July 1–16, 1992 106
An African Summit in Rome: August 4–7, 1992 111

6. Endgame 117

Military Questions: August 1992 118
Going to the Top for New Instructions: September 1–12, 1992 124
Summit Preview: September 13–25, 1992 130
Summit Finale: September 28 to October 4, 1992 134

Epilogue 141

Notes 149

Bibliography 153

Index 155

Foreword

Cameron Hume's case study of the Mozambique peace process deserves a wide readership and a place of distinction in the burgeoning literature on peacemaking in internal conflicts. Drawing upon his vantage point as the deputy chief of the U.S. mission to the Vatican, Hume offers a compelling analysis of how the Mozambicans made the peace accords of 1992. His chronicle is at once authoritative, conceptually lucid, and enlivened with a feel for the temperaments, appetites, fears, and human motives of the parties.

But Hume offers us much more than a contemporary diplomatic chronicle or an academic case study. For one thing, the presentation is accessible to a wide readership and is mercifully free of the deadening prose of bureaucracy or academe. For another, his professional grasp of both African affairs and the field of conflict resolution is impressive, so that the reader is in good hands on both accounts—a rare experience in such works. Serving at the core of a small network of U.S. officials whose assignments included the pursuit of peace in Mozambique, Hume writes as a participant-observer. And the story he tells is as special as his qualifications are for telling it.

Mozambique did not know real peace from 1961 to 1992. For most of that sad period, Mozambicans suffered horribly, as if they were plagued to live under an evil star. Governed by Europe's poorest empire and decolonized irresponsibly in great haste by Portugal after a long and costly anticolonial war, Mozambique had the ill-fortune to start out in 1975 under leaders who pursued the Afro-Marxist fantasies of that era. Worse, this vast, impoverished land was hurriedly abandoned by its 200,000-member

Portuguese community and then promptly became caught up in the Rhodesian (Zimbabwean) liberation struggle. Once Zimbabwe achieved independence in 1980, Mozambique became tragically trapped in the futile contest between the exiled African National Congress (ANC) and the South African Defence Forces. By the mid-1980s, sustained South African destabilization efforts in Mozambique had transformed the rebel movement RENAMO into a major military challenge to the FRELIMO regime; Mozambique had slipped into a brutal civil war that thrived on external involvement and on the many inadequacies of its incumbent government. It would be hard to imagine a less auspicious start to a country's independence.

Many outside parties—governments and non-governmental organizations—involved themselves in the country's internal affairs. None, however, had a strong enough incentive to become Mozambique's primary foreign "patron," and none was ideally suited to play such a role.

This backdrop helps explain a central feature of the Mozambican peace process whose origins go back to the mid-1980s but were formally launched in July 1990: its complex, if not bizarre, structure and the lead role played by non-state actors. Hume's book demonstrates how Italy (of all places) served as the host, venue, and inspired patron of Mozambican peacemaking in the 1990s. Hume gives us an authoritative account of the origins of the links between Mozambican church leaders, the Vatican, and especially the Community of Sant'Egidio—a Catholic lay order based in Rome's Trastevere district. His discussion of the origins and social-action commitments of this originally student-led group (which today has 10,000 members on four continents) sheds needed light on one of the most unusual mediation exercises in contemporary diplomacy.

For much of the active mediation phase, the mediation "team" comprised a Mozambican archbishop, an Italian socialist parliamentarian and former diplomat, and two key leaders of Sant'Egidio. At various stages, this exercise received the assistance of ten governments plus the UN secretary-general. Of the delicately named "observers," the Italian and U.S. governments were the most important, while Zimbabwe's President Robert Mugabe headed the list of key African leaders who worked to bring about the October 1992 settlement. (Other governmental actors included Britain, France, Portugal, Botswana, Kenya, Malawi, and South Africa). Finally, the book cites the special contributions of "Tiny" Rowland, the British-based and Africa-focused businessman who served as booster and kibbitzer as well as financier and travel agent for the parties at various points.

What is one to make of this idiosyncratic bouillabaisse of ingredients that made up the Mozambican peace process? Is it replicable? Can lessons be learned from it? Hume makes a persuasive case that useful conclusions can be drawn, and his detailed chronology is sprinkled with analytical asides that reflect the depth of his personal expertise while also explaining why the process unfolded as it did. The presence of non-state actors helped get around the "status" issue dividing the FRELIMO government led by President Joachim Chissano and the RENAMO rebel group led by Afonso Dhlakama. The Sant'Egidio mediation helped to transform this purely hostile relationship into a pattern of dialogue that over time led to an agenda and a series of protocols and accords.

But the Mozambique case is not by any means a pure case of "track two" negotiations. The discreet intervention of official diplomats was essential in formulating the sequence of issues to be addressed and defining a workable path forward on the military and constitutional issues. UN officials, in quiet coordination with key governments, made clear to the parties what would be necessary in order for the UN to oversee and help implement the necessary accords leading to encamping and demobilizing armed forces, forming a unified army, conducting an election campaign, monitoring the cease-fire, and other matters. Similarly, African and western governments (plus Rowland) were needed at various points in order to break through impasses among the heads of Mozambican delegations in Rome by appealing to the top leadership. Summitry was used to break logjams, set deadlines, create legitimacy, and force issues that might otherwise remain unresolved to this day.

Ending Mozambique's War will be a gold mine for scholars and practitioners seeking guidance on the "key factors" that led to the 1992 Mozambican accords. The answer will not fit on a bumper sticker. Clearly, the warring parties were nearing exhaustion, and this situation was reinforced by a devastating drought in 1992. By the early 1990s, no external party was prepared to keep sustaining its chosen Mozambican ally; alliances were frayed (for example, Zimbabwe wanted an exit from its intervention, and the Soviets and South Africans were disengaging), and donor fatigue had begun to appear; moreover, Mozambique had virtually no resources of its own to sustain the conflict. The impetus from Rome (both religious and official) found a receptive audience in southern Africa—in part because U.S., British, and Portuguese attention was directed elsewhere.

The skilled and deeply committed people of Sant'Egidio shaped history through their initial intervention, and as time passed, their efforts created a critical mass of facts and momentum so that there was something for "track one" decision-makers to support.

Indeed, this case offers dramatic support for the concept that third-party intervention can make the decisive difference, and that conflicts seldom resolve themselves (even when circumstances might appear propitious). Hume's account of the "endgame" that played out between August and October 1992 makes it abundantly clear that Chissano and Dhlakama needed constant "encouragement" to conclude what they had started. A week prior to the final Rome summit, Hume reports, the parties had "not seriously discussed" the key documents for putting the peace agreement into operation and had little understanding of what implementation would actually mean. They may have only dimly realized the full extent of what they agreed to during the subsequent four-day "working summit" that should be recorded as one of the most spontaneous summits of modern diplomacy.

As a result, the October 1992 accords are best understood as a decisive but not final stage in a peace process that continues to this day. Neither the UN system nor the Mozambican parties proved capable of adhering to the ambitious schedule laid down in Rome: in an act of realist statesmanship they mutually agreed to a full one-year delay of the implementation plan. If the October 1994 Mozambican elections produce a credible result, this will be further evidence for the proposition that peacemaking starts when a third-party actor gains the inspiration to intervene, and it does not end until all agreements have been implemented on the ground. The signing ceremony is but the beginning of the implementation phase—in some ways as crucial as any other. By the same token, the fact that the 1992 accords survived a one-year delay in implementation bears testimony to their quality and to the quality of the support they received from all concerned, as well as to the reality of Mozambique's readiness for peace.

Chester A. Crocker
Georgetown University

Preface

I wrote about these events from a specific vantage point. In December 1990, when I was visiting Washington to prepare for an assignment as deputy chief of mission at the U.S. embassy to the Holy See, Ambassador Herman J. Cohen, the assistant secretary of state for African affairs, asked me to carry on the work of my predecessor, James Creagan, with the Mozambique peace talks. I was to stay in touch with the mediators and the delegations of the Mozambican government and RENAMO in Rome, working to keep them engaged and, if possible, moving forward. Cohen emphasized that because the U.S. government had no other point of contact with RENAMO, I had to keep open the channel of communication in Rome.

Ten months later, Cohen's principal deputy assistant secretary, Ambassador Jeffrey Davidow, supplemented these instructions. After a working dinner with the mediators at the convent that serves as headquarters for the Community of Sant'Egidio, he told me to support the mediators, whether by offering them advice based on my previous experience with negotiations and peacekeeping or by planning and coordinating diplomatic approaches to the parties. Davidow informed the mediators of my new instructions, and they welcomed whatever support the United States could provide.

Thus for two years I met frequently with the two delegations, the mediators, and representatives of the other governments that eventually intervened in the negotiations. My position was at times on the outside of the negotiations, at other times on the fringe, never in the center. For an observer it was a good vantage point.

In July 1992 the United States Institute of Peace held a conference on regional conflicts. On the initiative of the Institute's president, former ambassador Samuel Lewis, and Professor Chester A. Crocker, I was invited to lead a panel discussing the conflict in Mozambique. Because of the conference participants' interest in the Mozambique peace process, I talked with Crocker about a book on the negotiations, which he encouraged me to write. When I returned to Rome, Ambassador Thomas P. Melady likewise encouraged me, as he often did during the two years of negotiations.

Three months later, after the general peace accord was signed on October 4, I was back in Washington with notes on the negotiations and an outline. Lewis said the United States Institute of Peace could provide a fellowship to facilitate the completion of a book, an offer that committed me to the project. David Smock, the Institute's coordinator for Africa, has since encouraged and advised me. At the same time, in response to a request from Hans Binnendijk and Margery Thompson at Georgetown University's Institute for the Study of Diplomacy, I began to write an article on the negotiations for *The Diplomatic Record 1992–93*.

I have examined those aspects of the negotiations with possible relevance for negotiations to bring other regional or local conflicts to an end. Because I had worked both in Washington and overseas on the problems of southern Africa, served in the Middle East, and been a member of the U.S. delegation to the United Nations, this focus seemed natural. This interest had already led me to write several articles and a book, *The United Nations, Iran, and Iraq: How Peacemaking Changed* (Indiana University Press, 1994).

Earlier, during the academic year 1989–90, while a fellow at Harvard's Center for International Affairs, I became involved with the work of the Harvard Negotiation Project (HNP). That work included an opportunity for me to join Professor Roger Fisher, Ambassador Viktor Issraelyan of the Diplomatic Academy of the USSR, and HNP staff members in conducting a training program on diplomatic negotiations at Columbia University for forty diplomats from more than twenty countries. The work done by Fisher and HNP provides a coherent framework for understanding even unorthodox negotiations, a framework that informed my own analysis at many points during the negotiations and later while writing.

I would like to thank the Johns Hopkins School for Advanced International Studies in Bologna for a workshop it hosted in March 1993. Faculty, students, members of the mediation team, and I explored the peace process with the benefit of hindsight. The workshop reinforced how important it is to distinguish the separate roles of the parties, the mediators, and the outside governments that intervened. That workshop deserves credit if this book succeeds in sharing the lessons of the Mozambique peace process with a wide range of readers.

Colleagues in the Department of State have given me wise counsel and support. In addition to Ambassadors Cohen and Davidow, I would like to mention members of the Africa Bureau's southern Africa negotiating team (John Byerly, Robert Cabelly, William Jackson, Randall Lecocq, Richard Roth, and Charles Snyder), as well as the U.S. ambassador in Maputo, Townsend B. Friedman, Jr.

The views expressed in this book are my own and do not necessarily represent those of the Department of State. For reasons of style, any mention of myself in the text is in the third person.

It would have been impossible to write this book without the friendship of members of the Community of Sant'Egidio. They have provided information that is available from no other source and shared their perspectives on what happened. I thank them.

The experience of building a durable peace in Mozambique should remind us all that negotiations must serve, above all, to change the character of relations between the parties. Formal written agreements are key milestones, showing both the distance already traveled and the road ahead. For peace to succeed in Mozambique, the government and RENAMO must have the courage to keep the peace process moving forward from their formal agreements, and the international community must have the wisdom to support their courage with generosity. May this happen elsewhere.

Ending Mozambique's War

MOZAMBIQUE

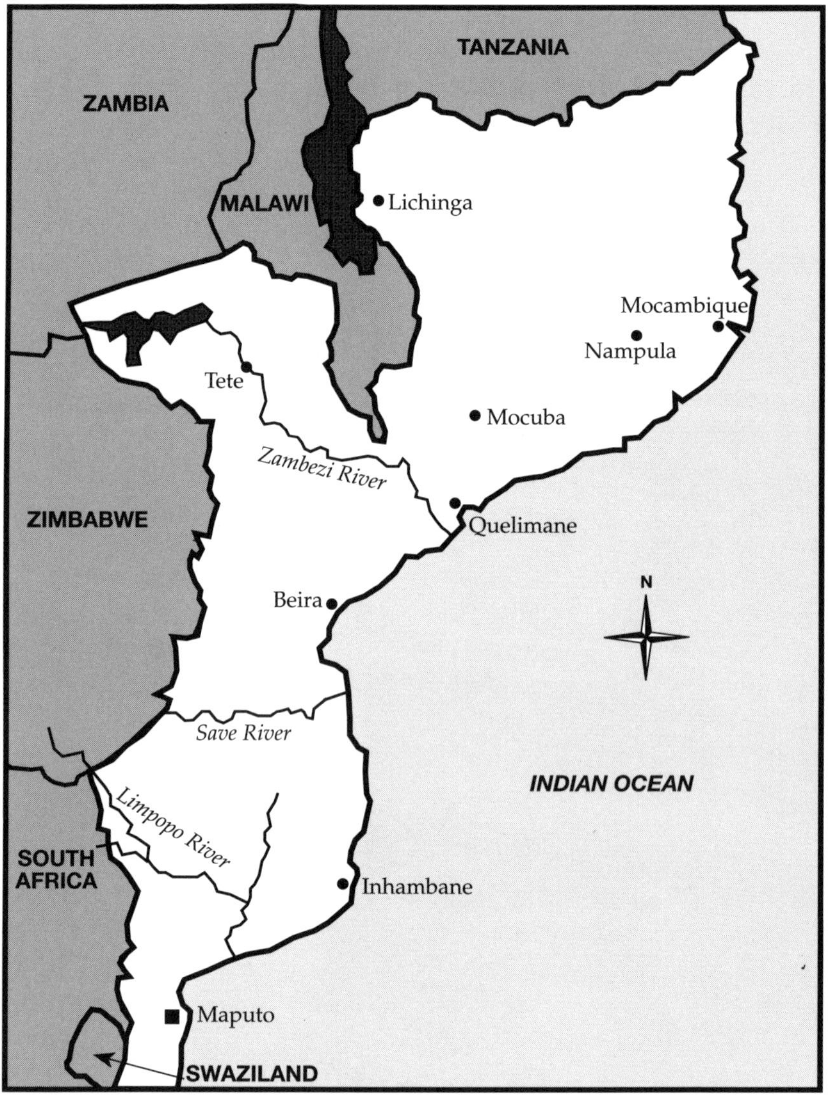

From *Maps on File*. ©1989 Martin Greenwald Associates. Reprinted with permission of Facts on File Inc., New York.

one

Seeds of Conflict

Mozambique, after gaining independence from Portugal in 1975, was battered by conflicts involving its neighbors, misled by its government's ideology, racked by insurgency, and devastated by drought. The government lacked the legitimacy, capacity, and stability to respond to these challenges. By 1990 the country desperately needed peace and reconciliation.

A photograph of the ceremony held on October 4, 1992, to celebrate the coming peace presents a tableau of traditional diplomacy that could have been arranged by central casting. Joaquim Chissano, president of Mozambique, and Afonso Dhlakama, president of RENAMO, had just signed an agreement to end the war of insurgency that RENAMO had waged against the government for fifteen years. The ceremony took place in the main conference room at the Farnesina, Italy's Foreign Ministry. Emilio Colombo, then Italy's foreign minister, presided. Next to him sat Chissano on one side and Dhlakama on the other. Along the dais, dignitaries were seated in what appears to be strict order of protocol: President Robert G. Mugabe of Zimbabwe; Sir Ketumile Masire, president of Botswana; Foreign Minister Roelof "Pik" Botha of South Africa; Secretary of State for Cooperation Jose Durao Barroso of Portugal; high officials from Zambia, Malawi, and Kenya; and UN Under Secretary-General James Jonah.

A second look reveals four other people seated at the head table: Mario Raffaelli, the Italian parliamentarian who led the team of mediators; Don Jaime Goncalves, archbishop of Beira; Professor Andrea Riccardi, president of the Community of Sant'Egidio; and Don Matteo Zuppi, a parish priest in Rome and a member of the Community of Sant'Egidio. The inclusion of these four mediators draws attention to a unique element in the Mozambique peace process: the role played by a private voluntary organization, the Community of Sant'Egidio.

Mozambique now had a new beginning. Conflicts among its neighbors were less acute; the government committed itself to replace a one-party state with a multiparty democracy; the rains returned; and the peace accord signalled the end of fighting. The team of mediators, operating outside the framework of traditional diplomacy, helped the parties along the path to peace and reconciliation. Could this experience have relevance for resolving other conflicts?

An Inauspicious Beginning

Before 1975 so much bad seed had been sown in Mozambique that the country would harvest the whirlwind: the wounds of centuries of Portuguese colonization, followed by a hasty, cut-and-run act of decolonization; the regional impact of heightened Cold War tensions; aggressive South African policies aimed at building bulwarks for white supremacy in southern Africa; and the extension to Mozambique of the armed struggle against minority white rule in Rhodesia. A less auspicious beginning for a new nation can hardly be imagined.

Foreign involvement in Mozambique dates from 1494, when Pope Alexander VI mediated the Treaty of Tordesillas between Spain and Portugal. This treaty stipulated that Portugal would have the right to land discovered in the hemisphere to the east of the forty-sixth meridian and Spain would have that right in the hemisphere to the west of the forty-sixth meridian. In 1498 the Portuguese arrived in Mozambique. For the next four centuries Portuguese settlers and traders concentrated along the coast, where they struggled to maintain control over the money economy and overseas commerce. At first gold and ivory and then, in the nineteenth century, slaves were the main commodities traded.[1] Most Mozambicans lived in traditional tribal societies, such as the Macua and Lomua in the north, the Sena and Ndau in the central region, and the Shangana in the south. The Portuguese presence in most of the country was minimal.

The Berlin Conference of 1885 established rules for the final European scramble to assert sovereignty over Africa. The conference decided that powers with settlements on the coast had priority for their claims over inland areas, but administrators or soldiers on the ground were needed to give substance to claims on a map. Portugal, which had scant resources to assert dominion over Mozambique (or Angola), counted on the support of the British government, which wanted to block German expansion from its colonies on the east and west coasts (now Tanzania and Namibia) and to protect the new British colony of Rhodesia.

At the beginning of the twentieth century the mining boom in South Africa and southern Rhodesia reinforced cooperation between Britain and Portugal in Mozambique. Mozambique, which stretches north to south along the coast for 2,400 kilometers (1,500 miles), was the natural outlet to the sea for most of the region. British capital developed ports and railroads to serve industries in South Africa and Rhodesia. The main rail lines were laid east to west from present-day Maputo to the Transvaal, from Beira to southern Rhodesia, and from Nacala to what is now Malawi. No rail line was built to run the length of the country. The Portuguese authorities granted agricultural and industrial concessions to British-backed firms and provided unskilled Mozambican labor to work in South African mines.

After fascism came to Portugal in 1932 the situation changed. The Salazar government asserted control over Portugal's African colonies to provide an outlet for Portuguese emigrants and a privileged domain for Lisbon's industrial, commercial, and financial enterprises. Portugal increased its share of Mozambique's trade to more than half the colony's total, and the European population climbed from less than 30,000 in 1930 to more than 200,000 by 1975.[2] But the essential character of Portuguese colonialism changed little. Europeans concentrated in commercial towns along the coast, and the colonial authorities cooperated with traditional tribal leaders in the hinterlands. Aside from church schools, there was practically no education for blacks and few opportunities for advancement in a labor market dominated by semi-skilled Portuguese emigrants. Certainly there were no plans to prepare the country for independence.

In the 1960s, winds of change were blowing across Africa. On September 23, 1960, Nikita S. Khrushchev, then chairman of the Council of Ministers of the USSR, told the UN General Assembly that the time had come for the "complete and final liberation of peoples languishing in colonial bondage." Three months later the General Assembly, to eradicate the diplomatic sanction for European colonialism in Africa provided first by the Treaty of Tordesillas and then by the Berlin Conference, adopted resolution 1514 (XV), which stated that "the subjection of peoples to alien subjugation, domination, and exploitation constitutes a denial of fundamental human rights, is contrary to the Charter of the United Nations, and is an impediment to the promotion of world peace and co-operation." France, Portugal,

South Africa, the United Kingdom, and the United States were among the nine delegations not supporting the resolution.

In 1974, after a run of more than four decades, Portuguese fascism collapsed. Portugal, unable to adapt to demands for change at home and battered by uprisings in its African colonies, had become a relic at the edge of a modernizing Europe. The new authorities in Lisbon decided to grant Mozambique independence as soon as possible, even though Portugal had done nothing to prepare the country for independence. White fright and then flight of as many as 200,000 Portuguese settlers deprived Mozambique of administrators, merchants, professionals, tradespeople, and most skilled and semi-skilled workers. After 477 years of colonial rule, Portugal left Mozambique in a shambles.

In 1975, when Mozambique became independent, Cold War tensions were at a peak. As usual, calm reigned on the central fronts in Europe and Northeast Asia; armed clashes were more likely to involve proxies on the periphery in southeast Asia, the Middle East, Central America, or southern Africa. In 1975, fighting took place in Angola.

After the new government in Lisbon committed itself to immediate independence for Angola and Mozambique, South Africa changed its security strategy. South Africa had previously counted on Portuguese rule in Angola and Mozambique as a bulwark to stop the consequences of decolonization from reaching South Africa. Deprived of a white-ruled buffer zone stretching across Angola, Rhodesia, and Mozambique, the South African government adopted a forward defense based on its ability to project power beyond South Africa's borders. The government preferred to rely on local insurgent forces dependent on South African support, but it was willing to send South African troops if need be. South Africa implemented this new strategy first in Angola.

In January 1975 Portugal signed an agreement with the three Angolan liberation groups for elections to be held before independence on November 11, 1975. Fighting flared up between the three groups: Holden Roberto's Frente Nacional da Libertacao de Angola (FNLA), based in the north, received external support from President Mobutu Sese Seko of Zaire, from western countries, and from China; Agostinho Neto's Movimento Popular da Libertacao de Angola (MPLA), an avowedly Marxist-Leninist group based more in urban areas, had support from Communist bloc countries and Cuba; Jonas Savimbi's Uniao Nacional para a Independencia Total de Angola (UNITA), based in the southern half of the country, benefited from strong tribal loyalties and external support from South Africa and some western countries. Admiral Rosa Coutinho, in charge of the Portuguese administration in Luanda, opposed elections and wanted to transfer power directly to the MPLA. To this end he facilitated the delivery of arms and the arrival of Cuban military advisers and combat troops. In late summer MPLA forces moved south along the coast, and by October, Cuban forces were arriving in substantial numbers.[3]

The South African Defense Forces (SADF) first intervened to protect a hydroelectric installation that provided water and electric power to Namibia. By Angola's independence day, a South African armored column had advanced half the distance from Angola's border with Namibia to Luanda, stopping on the coast north of Benguela. In military terms the SADF advance was a remarkable feat of daring; in political terms it accomplished little. The South Africans got no support in the West for their campaign to stop what they claimed was a Communist onslaught against all southern Africa. The MPLA, backed by the Soviet Union and Cuba but not sanctioned by elections, held on to power in Luanda.

For another ten years the situation changed little. The FNLA was defeated and faded away. The MPLA, backed by Soviet aid and Cuban soldiers, ruled in Luanda. UNITA, protected by the South African military based in northern Namibia and then backed by the United States, controlled southern Angola.

The struggle for black rule in Rhodesia had a greater impact on Mozambique. The theater of military operations included areas of Mozambique where the forces of Robert Mugabe's Zimbabwe African National Union (ZANU) took refuge. Many Zimbabweans, including Mugabe, are members of the Shona ethnic group, which extends across the border in central Mozambique. The transport lines that link the economies of the two countries had brought relative prosperity to the port of Beira in Mozambique, which was an important outlet to the sea for Rhodesian commerce. South Africa, which shared a common border with Rhodesia, had a security interest in Rhodesia comparable to Britain's at the time of the Berlin Conference.

Mozambique's independence in 1975 made a difference for the Rhodesian conflict. The new government in Maputo applied the UN economic sanctions against Rhodesia, cutting off Rhodesia's access to the port of Beira. ZANU forces were now assured of sanctuary inside Mozambique, making it more difficult for the Rhodesian forces to control the border area. Perhaps most important, the independence of Angola and Mozambique, by identifying Rhodesia as the "next" country to achieve black majority rule in southern Africa, had an enormous psychological impact on both sides in the war.

FRELIMO

The Frente da Libertacao de Mocambique (FRELIMO) was founded in 1962 at a meeting in Dar es Salaam. Its founders elected Eduardo Mondlane, who had received a doctorate in anthropology from Northwestern University and whose wife was American, to be FRELIMO's first president. In 1964 FRELIMO launched its armed struggle to secure the independence of Mozambique from Portugal.

There were tensions within FRELIMO's leadership. The dominant faction, many of whose leaders came from tribes in the south of the country, favored a radical revolutionary policy that aimed not only to defeat the Portuguese but also to liberate the people from traditional authorities. This faction wanted to restructure society along the lines of scientific socialism. The other faction gave priority to taking over from the Portuguese and developing a new generation of leaders, which at the time meant education abroad for a new elite that might not have the experience of the armed struggle.[4] This faction's most prominent leaders were Lazaro Nkavandame, a traditional leader from the north of the country, and Matteus Gwenjere, a Catholic priest from Beira. In 1968 the FRELIMO headquarters in Dar es Salaam was sacked during riots. In 1969 a parcel bomb killed Mondlane.

One month later FRELIMO elected Samora Machel, the candidate of the more radical faction, to succeed Mondlane. Machel was a former nurse turned military commander. FRELIMO insurgent forces, backed by the Soviet Union and China, soon expanded their presence in the northern part of the country, where they were closer to their logistics base in Tanzania. By 1973 they had reached the central part of the country near the Beira corridor. The Portuguese, despite their overwhelming superiority in sophisticated weapons, could not protect the country from an insurgency that relied on light weapons and land mines.

After the April 1974 coup in Lisbon, Portuguese authorities proposed for Mozambique a transition period that would include elections before independence. FRELIMO insisted that, as the "sole legitimate representative of the Mozambican people," it should take over power directly without any elections being held. In September Portugal gave up its insistence on elections and agreed to hand over power to FRELIMO after a nine-month transition. Samora Machel traveled abroad during this period to bolster his international stature, including one trip to China, where he visited Chou En-lai in a Beijing hospital,[5] and another to Britain.[6]

On June 25, 1975, Samora Machel was sworn in as Mozambique's first president. In his inauguration speech Machel promised a non-racial, anti-capitalist policy: "We do not recognize tribes, regions, race, or religious belief. . . . We only recognize Mozambicans who are equally exploited and equally desirous of freedom and revolution."[7] FRELIMO's announced policy was to create a modernized, disciplined, socialist country.

The Soviet Union recognized the new republic in time for Soviet president Nikolai Podgorny to attend the inauguration ceremonies. Diplomatic relations with the United States would have to wait six months.

For the next five years Machel moved Mozambique down FRELIMO's chosen path. FRELIMO sought legitimacy by proclaiming itself a vanguard party that would protect the revolution and promote development. The government removed or subjugated traditional local authorities who had been left in place during the centuries of Portuguese colonialism. The government nationalized private homes, rental property, other private land holdings, the practice of medicine or law, and educational institutions. Despite its lack of trained or experienced personnel, the government assumed responsibility for managing nationalized enterprises and farms and tried to replace the market with a system of administered prices. Eastern bloc technicians arrived to train Mozambican bureaucrats. These policy choices deprived private initiative of any reward, retarded community development, and concentrated power in the hands of a central government unprepared to exercise it.

In foreign policy, Machel's initial moves went in the same direction. In May 1976 he visited the Soviet Union for six days. On April 1, 1977, he and Nikolai Podgorny signed a treaty of friendship between Mozambique and the Soviet Union. In February 1979 East German president Erich Honecker came to Maputo for a three-day visit. By the end of that year, 200 Cuban military advisers were working with the Mozambican Armed Forces (FAM). In November 1980, at the end of another visit to the Soviet Union, Machel endorsed a joint statement that aligned Mozambique with all Moscow's foreign policy.

The most pressing security question facing Machel's government was the war in Rhodesia to end rule by Ian Smith's white minority regime. Machel's government had closed the Beira corridor to Rhodesian commerce, and from bases in western Mozambique Mugabe's ZANU units stepped up pressure on the Rhodesians. To retaliate the Rhodesians attacked areas inside Mozambique, including infrastructure targets such as bridges, dams, and railroads. Then in 1977 the Smith regime created a new instrument of retaliation: Rhodesian military intelligence helped to found the Mozambican insurgent movement called the Mozambican National Resistance (MNR); subsequently the name was changed to Resistencia Nacional Mocambicana (RENAMO).[8] The Rhodesians wanted RENAMO to provide intelligence on ZANU operations and to keep pressure on Machel's government.

In 1979, shortly after Margaret Thatcher became British prime minister, she endorsed a plan by her foreign secretary, Lord Peter Carrington, to seek a negotiated solution to the war in Rhodesia. Thatcher's government convened negotiations in London at Lancaster House on a proposal including a quick cease-fire, constitutional guarantees for minority rights, a brief transition period administered by British authorities, an early election, and internationally recognized independence. Carrington convinced the Rhodesian parties, black and white, to accept the broad lines of his plan and to work out the details needed for implementation. No country had been more affected than Mozambique by the war in Rhodesia, and the formal transfer of power to Zimbabwe's new government in 1980 was a sign of hope for Mozambique as well. When Zimbabwe's new president, Robert G. Mugabe, visited Maputo in December 1981, Machel made him an honorary citizen of Mozambique.

Machel's government could now concentrate on domestic policy. At the beginning of the 1980s, drought and the world recession were battering the agricultural sector, and the government's insistence on one-party rule and state control of the economy made the situation worse.

The epitome of the government's domestic policy was Operation Production. Deputy Interior Minister Teodato Hunguana described the program's purpose: "We want this [Maputo] to be a clean city, a productive city, not a city of parasites."[9] In 1983 the government deported 50,000 unemployed from the cities (30,000 from Maputo alone) to the countryside with orders that they farm. Military brigades rounded up potential deportees, most of whom were summarily transported to the north. The campaign kept forty courts working round the clock just to hear those cases in which the authorities admitted there might be some doubt. Hunguana complained that it was difficult to make people understand that they were not being punished but only being sent to the countryside to help with the country's development. In 1983 alone an estimated 100,000 people starved to death in the drought regions.[10] This policy initiative bore the earmarks of scientific socialism.

In these years the RENAMO insurgency was the main security threat facing FRELIMO. The government's domestic policies had alienated large segments of the population through political repression and economic failure, making it easier for RENAMO to round up recruits. The FAM—although now equipped and trained by Communist bloc governments to use jet aircraft, artillery, and tanks—was no more capable than the Portuguese army of controlling a rural insurgency that used foot soldiers, light weapons, and land mines. To cut off external support for RENAMO, Machel decided to negotiate an agreement with South Africa, whose security policy was still driven by the claimed threat of a "total onslaught" by Communist states against southern Africa and whose security services had become a source of support for RENAMO. Although RENAMO never identified its sources of external support, it was widely suspected that they also included some Portuguese and South African business interests.

In March 1984, during meetings in Maputo and Cape Town, the two sides thrashed out the text of a non-aggression pact. The head of Mozambique's delegation, General Jacinto Soares Veloso, said, "The essential point of the agreement is that my country will not serve as a base for attacks or violence against the territory of South Africa and vice versa."[11] South African President P. W. Botha and Machel met at the town where the Nkomati River crosses the border to sign the agreement. Botha promised that South African support for RENAMO would end, and Machel that Mozambique would not give military support to the African National Congress (ANC), which Pretoria claimed was the local agent of the Communist onslaught.

Mozambique closed the ANC offices in Maputo, but South Africa did not cut off its aid to RENAMO. Indeed, documents found in 1985 at RENAMO's Gorongosa headquarters in central Mozambique showed that some South African support continued.[12]

After its first decade in office the Machel government adjusted course from the Marxist-Leninist rhetoric that dominated its early policy choices. In 1985 a U.S. Department of State's human rights report struggled to put FRELIMO's record in the best possible light by comparing it with what the Portuguese had done or to the atrocities being committed by RENAMO. The report described FRELIMO as a "self-proclaimed nationalist and Marxist-Leninist party" that was becoming more pragmatic. However, the small group of senior officials headed by Machel still controlled the party, and the government allowed no opposition political activity. "There is little tolerance for public criticism of basic government policies and officials at the national level. . . . The Government controls all authorized publications in the country, as well as the radio and experimental television facilities. . . . Since political opposition to the Government and to FRELIMO ideology is not permitted, public gatherings of all but a purely social nature are controlled by the local authorities."[13]

There were two separate legal systems: one administered by the minister of the interior and the other by the state security service (SNASP). SNASP had jurisdiction over "political crimes against the State and economic sabotage." SNASP had in the past held detainees indefinitely without formal charges. The report estimated neither the number of persons detained for political reasons nor the number who had earlier been detained in the re-education camps. Obviously even pragmatic Marxism-Leninism could produce massive human rights violations.

The report identified areas in which improvements had occurred. Torture was still a problem, but since a formal judiciary had been established in 1979, the number of prisoners at re-education camps who were bound, beaten, and often killed had decreased. In 1981 Machel declared that prisoners would be sent to such camps only after due process. Operation Production had not been repeated, leading to a drop in arrests, even if detainees were still held incommunicado for long periods. Repression of religion—which had included confiscation of church properties, including schools, clinics, and places of worship—was easing, and Catholic bishops' pastoral letters that criticized government policies now circulated without reprisals.

The economic situation was still a disaster and getting worse. Since 1980 the economy had shrunk each year—by 18 percent during Operation Production in 1983. Between 1980 and 1985, port traffic, export crops, and industrial production fell by more than half, and foreign debt almost tripled. The volume of exports of key cash crops dropped from almost 800,000 tons in 1981 to little more than 150,000 tons in 1986. Per capita gross national product, which had been almost $400 at the beginning of the decade, was heading toward $100 by the decade's end. Drought in the agricultural areas and the depredations of RENAMO throughout the country made this disaster worse, but the FRELIMO leadership bore the responsibility for the consequences of its own policy choices.

In September 1985 Machel visited Washington. When he met with President Reagan, Machel explained that despite South Africa's bad faith in supplying RENAMO contrary to the Nkomati Accord, his government would maintain its commitment.[14] Machel's government had already shifted toward closer economic and security relations with the West, and it was trying to rethink its domestic policies. After the meeting President Reagan told Secretary of State Shultz, "I don't want to sound naive, but I think that guy is sincere."[15]

On October 19, 1986, Machel died in a plane crash inside South Africa. He left behind a country still suffering from its government's policies, from civil war, and from deepening poverty.

Within two weeks the FRELIMO central committee elected Joaquim Chissano to replace Machel as president of Mozambique and as head of FRELIMO. In the election within the politburo, Chissano had defeated Armando Emilio Guebuza, the minister of the interior who had directed Operation Production and who was the candidate of the more radical faction in the party. Chissano, a member of the Shangana tribe in the south, had studied in Paris before independence and spoke French, Portuguese, and English fluently. He had learned the virtues of flexibility and pragmatism as foreign minister. Chissano lacked Machel's charisma and took a more intellectual, studied approach to issues, at times giving the impression that he was mired in details. Within a year of taking office, on October 7, 1987, Chissano met with President Reagan at the White House.

RENAMO

RENAMO's first leader was Andre Matsangaissa. In the early days many RENAMO recruits had previous military experience, some from serving with the former Portuguese forces in Mozambique and others, like Matsangaissa, from serving with FRELIMO. Matsangaissa died in 1979 during an attack on a government position in the Gorongosa game park in central Mozambique, an area that later became RENAMO's headquarters. Afonso Dhlakama became RENAMO's second leader.[16]

Dhlakama was from central Mozambique. Unlike Mondlane, Machel, and Chissano, who all came from the Shangana tribe in the south, he belonged to the small Ndau tribe, which in turn is a subgroup of the Shona, the largest ethnic group in Zimbabwe. Perhaps because his father was a Ndau chief, he resented FRELIMO's policy of destroying traditional authority structures.[17] His only formal education was at a rural Catholic mission school, and he lacked the political polish that marked FRELIMO's leadership.

Other RENAMO leaders inside Mozambique came from a rural background and lacked the educational advantages of the government's leaders. Raul Domingos, a member of the Sena tribe allied to the Ndau, was recruited into the movement while a teenager, then was trained by Rhodesians and South Africans, and later became a senior military commander. Vicente Ululu studied in a church school and then in a teacher training program in Tanzania; he became Dhlakama's senior civilian adviser, speech writer, and English teacher. Expatriate Mozambicans in western capitals, operating as freelance volunteers, claimed to represent RENAMO overseas, but they rarely had direct personal relations with Dhlakama and the cadres serving under his command. RENAMO's external relations were ill coordinated.

South Africa became RENAMO's chief outside patron after Zimbabwe's independence in 1979. South African support consisted primarily of providing training, small arms and ammunition, medical supplies, and communication equipment. To help RENAMO leaders establish or maintain external relations, South Africa provided introductions and transportation. Rumors abounded that Portuguese business interests that had lost properties in Mozambique after independence supported RENAMO, but RENAMO spokesmen always denied any connection. RENAMO troops, recruited inside Mozambique, maintained themselves by raiding the civilian population for food and by capturing military supplies from the government's forces. Although the South African government promised in the 1984 Nkomati Accord to stop its patronage of RENAMO, the covert relationship continued.

In October 1984 Pretoria hosted an abortive round of discussions between the government and RENAMO aimed at producing a cease-fire.[18] When it seemed that an agreement might be reached, elements of the South African government and Portuguese business interests prompted the RENAMO representatives to break off the talks.[19] A South African connection could never give RENAMO the kind of political credibility that the United States provided for the UNITA movement in Angola.

As late as 1985, when RENAMO was stepping up its attacks, it remained a shadowy organization with a rudimentary structure. Dhlakama headed both military and civilian wings. The military, numbering about 12,000 in 1985, was organized into northern, central, and southern zones. Dhlakama planned and directed major military campaigns, but surely many RENAMO attacks were local initiatives. The RENAMO forces were less well equipped than the FAM, but they often bested the FAM in intelligence, command and control, morale, initiative, and tactics.

RENAMO's human rights practices earned it a baneful reputation as the "Khmer Rouge" of Africa. RENAMO targets were civilian targets, whether economic infrastructure or civilian settlements that could be pillaged to supply its forces. Civilians might be tortured, maimed, murdered—or perhaps kidnapped, enlisted, and later released. RENAMO's targets were frequently in the transport corridors, but RENAMO's brand of terror was present throughout the country. For example, in April 1985 RENAMO ambushed civilian convoys traveling between Maputo and nearby Gaza Province, killing more than 200 civilians, some by bayonet.[20] On occasion RENAMO kidnapped and held foreigners, including missionaries and humanitarian assistance workers. A controversial report submitted to the State Department by Robert Gersony in 1988 stated that RENAMO's violence against civilians included "shooting executions, knife/axe/bayonet killings, burying alive, beating to death, forced asphyxiation, forced starvation, forced drownings, and random shooting at civilians in villages during attacks."[21] Gersony's report eliminated any chance RENAMO might have had for U.S. support.

Those who investigated RENAMO's practices reached these harsh judgments after a serious study of the facts.[22] RENAMO representatives criticized these judgments bitterly, but they offered no basis for reaching different conclusions. As yet RENAMO had neither an articulated ideology nor an organizational structure through which its views could be explained.

The Community of Sant'Egidio

On February 7, 1968, at the beginning of a year that in Italy became a symbol of rebellion against the old order, a group of students met at Rome's Virgil High School to found a voluntary charitable organization through which they could express a commitment to society. Most student groups in Italy took their inspiration from the ideologies of the Marxist left; the students about to found the Community of Sant'Egidio explicitly took inspiration from their Christian faith. They described their purpose as spreading the truth of the Gospel. The founders wanted to work along the lines of change laid down during Vatican Council II, with a special emphasis on dialogue with followers of other religions and on work with the poor. The organizational structure of Sant'Egidio would recall the lay confraternities that were so active in Renaissance Italy.

Andrea Riccardi has been Sant'Egidio's leader since its founding. In 1980 he became at the age of thirty the youngest full professor in Italy, and he has since taught ecclesiastical history at Rome's Sapienza University. He has published books on Gallicanism in France in the nineteenth century, on the church of Pius XII, on the powers of the popes, on the Vatican's relations with Moscow, on the city of Rome, and on the church and the papacy in the contemporary world. He is a regular contributor to the Vatican's *Osservatore Romano*.

Matteo Zuppi, a younger student at the Virgil High School, joined Sant'Egidio in 1971 and later became a priest. His father was a journalist for the *Osservatore Romano*, and his mother's uncle, Cardinal Confalonieri, had been Pope Pius XI's secretary of state. He became deputy parish priest at Santa Maria in Trastevere, a neighborhood that for more than 2,000 years has been a crossroads for the meeting of different classes and nationalities. Santa Maria is a twelfth-century basilica built over the remains of a barracks for Roman legionnaires, a site that has been a place of Christian worship since the third century and is the burial place for five early popes. Don Matteo used his naturally outgoing personality to develop special ties to parishioners in greatest need: the poor, Gypsies, addicts, orphans, AIDS victims, and the handicapped. He led Sant'Egidio's group that sought ways to express solidarity with the Third World through activities in countries as diverse as Albania, Argentina, Ethiopia, Guatemala, Mexico, Mozambique, Somalia, and Vietnam.

Sant'Egidio has close relations with the Holy See and with Pope John Paul II. For its headquarters the Community was given a sixteenth-century former Carmelite convent around the corner from Santa Maria in Trastevere. The convent, including its small chapel, was built by the Colonna family, Roman nobles with ties to the Renaissance popes. The Italian government restored and converted the convent into a maze of reception areas, meeting rooms, and offices.

Several times each year, Pope John Paul II meets with Sant'Egidio's leaders, and on occasion he invites its members to his private mass. In 1986 he granted Sant'Egidio a special status, specifying a vocation that focuses on bringing Christianity to those furthest from the experience of a practicing religion, on ecumenical dialogue with other religions, and on service to the poor.

As part of Sant'Egidio's ecumenical mission, its members organized on October 27, 1986, in Assisi a day of prayer for world peace. From all over the world hundreds of religious leaders gathered in the Umbrian countryside at the birthplace of Saint Francis. Three years later, at the suggestion of Poland's Cardinal Josef Glemp, whose titular church in Rome is Santa Maria in Trastevere, Sant'Egidio members organized with the Polish government a day of prayer for peace in Warsaw to commemorate the fiftieth anniversary of the outbreak of the Second World War.[23] In the years since, Sant'Egidio has organized similar meetings each fall. In January 1993 the Holy See used this format for the day of prayer and fasting that the pope convened in Assisi for the purpose of peace in the Balkans. On that occasion members of Sant'Egidio provided the hospitality for Muslim and Jewish religious leaders who participated.

The Community of Sant'Egidio now has more than 10,000 members worldwide and 300 local groups in numerous Italian cities, in other European countries, in Latin America, and in Africa. Community members provide social services to children at risk, immigrants, the poor, the old, and the infirm. Sant'Egidio members staff schools and clinics in the Third World. They are the foremost provider of assistance to the homeless in Rome.

Sant'Egidio's commitment to tolerance and dialogue has led it, unlike many other charitable or voluntary organizations, to engage in political activity. For example, during a 1982 meeting at Sant'Egidio's headquarters, the Lebanese Druze leader Walid Jumblatt and the patriarch of the Lebanese Melichites, Maximos V, signed an agreement to stop the war between Christians and Druze in the Shuf Mountains south of Beirut. Sant'Egidio members organize—at times with other civic organizations such as labor unions—conferences and demonstrations to mobilize public opinion against racism, anti-Semitism, and intolerance. Sant'Egidio's leaders have extensive contacts with Italian politicians and officials.

The ties between Sant'Egidio and Mozambique go back to 1976, when a young Mozambican priest studying in Rome, Don Jaime Goncalves, became a friend of Sant'Egidio members. A year later Goncalves, recently named the archbishop of Beira, returned to Rome for a synod. He explained to his friends at Sant'Egidio the problems of the Christian churches in Mozambique. In the first years of independence the FRELIMO government confiscated some church properties, closed church schools and clinics, and imposed restrictions on religious leaders. At one point Goncalves was imprisoned for six months.

Members of Sant'Egidio looked for ways to remove the restrictions on religious freedom in Mozambique. Eventually, they introduced Archbishop Goncalves to Senator Gerardo Chiaromonte, a hard-line Communist who led the Italian Communist Party in Trastevere. After Don Jaime recounted his story of repression of religion in Mozambique, Chiaromonte responded that FRELIMO was wrong to suppress the Roman Catholic Church. As he explained to the startled archbishop, Mozambique first had to pass through the phase of Christianity before it would be prepared for Communism. In 1981 Andrea Riccardi organized a meeting between Enrico Berlinguer, then head of the Italian Communist Party, and members of the Community interested in Mozambique, including Goncalves. Berlinguer offered to use his own moral authority and the weight of the fraternal party support given by the Italian Communists to persuade FRELIMO to remove restrictions against the practice of religion.

These contacts opened a dialogue between the government in Maputo and members of Sant'Egidio. Berlinguer maintained his interest in Mozambique—as late as ten days before his death in 1984, he interrupted an election campaign to fly back to Rome to meet with Goncalves at Sant'Egidio.

Members of Sant'Egidio worked to meet Mozambique's humanitarian needs as well. Andrea Riccardi and Don Matteo Zuppi went to Maputo in 1984 to discuss humanitarian needs with government ministers. They made contact with Italian foreign minister Giulio Andreotti and with Mario Raffaelli, who for six years during the 1980s was an under-secretary at the Italian Foreign Ministry, to gain government support for programs set up by Sant'Egidio to deliver food and medicine. In 1985 Sant'Egidio sent Mozambique a "ship of solidarity" with 3,500 tons of humanitarian aid, and in 1988 a second ship arrived with 7,000 tons. Sant'Egidio developed a network of committees in Italy to obtain funds and material for Mozambique and to spread information in Europe on Mozambique's crisis. A parallel network soon appeared inside Mozambique, often as part of the local parishes, to help orphans, students, and others suffering from the war. Two Sant'Egidio members were killed in Mozambique during armed attacks.

Sant'Egidio members developed ties to missionaries in Mozambique, who often served in the no-man's-land or in the war zones controlled by RENAMO. In 1982 representatives of Sant'Egidio, perhaps helped by the fact that Goncalves came from the same area as Dhlakama, negotiated the release of priests and nuns being held by RENAMO. As a result, Sant'Egidio began to develop a relationship of credibility and trust with the insurgents.

Sant'Egidio facilitated contacts between the Mozambican government and the Holy See. Several times Archbishop Achille Sylvestrini, then the Vatican's foreign minister, visited Sant'Egidio headquarters for quiet, informal meetings with government representatives. On one occasion he arranged for the government to release an Italian friar, Giocondo Pagliara, who had been arrested under a charge of being a "treasurer" for RENAMO. In 1985 President Machel intended to stop in Rome on his return from meeting with President Reagan in Washington and from addressing the UN General Assembly in New York. Machel let it be known that he wanted to meet the pope, but he refused to make a formal request for such a meeting, as Holy See protocol requires. Sant'Egidio found a way to bridge the gap. Although the pope and Machel did not resolve any of the specific problems barring establishment of diplomatic relations between the two sides, their meeting broke down the wall of suspicion and gave further impetus to Machel's turn toward dialogue as the only way to solve Mozambique's problems.[24]

Outsiders

Mozambique's dependence on outsiders grew throughout its first decade of independence. Because of the war against RENAMO, the government turned to outside governments first to supply arms and advisers to the FAM, then to provide military units to protect the transport corridors, and later to join in attacks on RENAMO. Because of the disastrous economic situation, the government needed assistance from the International Monetary Fund (IMF) and the World Bank (International Bank for Reconstruction and Development), from other international agencies, and from individual donor governments. As outsiders became more involved, they developed an interest in ending the war.

The Soviet Union was the main source of outside support for the FAM. The FAM was composed of ground forces (approximately 35,000 army, 5,000 border guards, and 15,000 militia), a small navy (probably less than 2,000), and an air force (several thousand, divided into air force and air defense units). At one time Moscow supplied jet planes, tanks, and other heavy equipment, but by 1986 it was providing fewer heavy weapons, and the yearly value of its arms supplies dropped from more than $600 million to less than $200 million. The Soviet Union and Cuba each sent in more than 500 military advisers or trainers. Despite this external support, the FAM never excelled as a military force, and it made no headway against the insurgents.

Three of Mozambique's neighbors provided military units. Tanzania sent more than 3,000 troops to help out in heavily populated Zambezia Province. Malawi sent a battalion of less than 1,000 troops to protect the rail line in the Nacala corridor in the northern part of the country. Zimbabwean forces provided security for the Beira corridor, and they were active in the Limpopo corridor in the south and along the Tete corridor road in the north linking Zimbabwe and Malawi. Mugabe's decision to deploy more than 5,000 Zimbabwean troops repaid the fraternal help FRELIMO had given to ZANU forces during the struggle for Zimbabwe's independence. Zimbabwe's army, unlike the FAM, was disciplined and well led. From time to time these troops participated in operations outside the transport corridors. In August 1985 a joint Zimbabwean-FAM force based in the Beira corridor conducted a major operation to capture

RENAMO's headquarters at Gorongosa. In the months that followed the base changed hands several times, but eventually RENAMO re-established possession.[25]

South Africa was RENAMO's only significant source of outside military support. Compared with either the volume of material sent to the FAM by its Communist bloc friends or the number of troops provided by neighboring states, this support was minimal. RENAMO simply captured most of its equipment and supplies from the FAM. South African military intelligence, led by Major General Cornelius van Tonder, trained troops and provided communications equipment; RENAMO became superior to the FAM in intelligence, command and control, and leadership of small units. As FRELIMO had shown in its fight against the Portuguese army, a determined insurgency relying on foot soldiers, light weapons, and land mines could score easily in the countryside against a traditional, heavily armed force.

Outsiders became involved in efforts to rescue the economy. In the aftermath of FRELIMO's fourth party congress in 1983 and the disastrous Operation Production, the government's economic policy shifted emphasis from large state projects to smaller, market-oriented projects.[26] In 1984 Mozambique joined the IMF and the World Bank. In 1987 the government adopted an economic reform program along the lines of IMF-sanctioned austerity measures: devaluation of the currency, reductions in the state sector, cuts in subsidy programs, more fiscal responsibility, and a greater role for the private sector. Western creditors rescheduled repayments on $1.6 billion of Mozambique's debt to western lenders, and foreign aid disbursements went up from little more than $200 million in 1986 to almost $900 million by 1988. In 1988 the largest donors were, in order, Italy, Sweden, the IMF and the World Bank, the United States, the European Economic Community, the Netherlands, the Soviet Union, the United Kingdom, nongovernmental organizations, France, Norway, and Canada. Only this massive infusion of foreign aid saved the economy from total collapse, with further devastating consequences for the Mozambican people.

U.S. Assistant Secretary of State Chester A. Crocker, during testimony before the Senate Foreign Relations Committee on June 24, 1987, described the change in Mozambique's policy from military dependence on the Communist bloc to closer ties with other states.[27] This testimony was part of Crocker's successful effort to unblock the confirmation of Melissa Wells as the next U.S. ambassador to Mozambique. He explained that, following a meeting between Secretary of State Shultz and then foreign minister

Chissano in 1982, the Mozambican government had cooperated with Crocker's marathon effort to negotiate Namibia's independence and the withdrawal of Cuban troops from Angola. The September 1985 meeting between President Reagan and President Machel gave new impetus to this cooperation and encouraged the Mozambican government to shift domestic policies. Changes began to appear in economic policy, and restrictions on religious freedom were lifted.

Crocker told the senators that President Chissano, on his first trip abroad as president, had met with Prime Minister Thatcher on May 6, 1987, for what the British described as "exceptionally warm" talks. The British, who were now training FAM troops, announced they would increase both the training program and their level of economic assistance. Chissano went on to Rome, where he met with the pope and with President Francesco Cossiga, Prime Minister Amintore Fanfani, and Foreign Minister Giulio Andreotti. The Italians announced a cancellation of Mozambican debt and an increase in their assistance program.

As for RENAMO, Crocker said that it "lacks a credible political identity where it really counts—in Mozambique itself." Although the United States would not hesitate to promote contacts between the government and RENAMO for the purpose of ending hostilities, Crocker cautioned that "Mozambicans themselves must be the primary architects of a peaceful future for their country."

Two months after he met with President Reagan in October 1987, President Chissano proclaimed an amnesty program to begin on January 1, 1988. Insurgents who turned themselves in to the government were guaranteed protection from prosecution, and they would be welcomed back into normal society by public ceremonies. During the next year approximately 3,000 took advantage of this program[28]—a figure large enough to demonstrate a desire for reconciliation, but hardly enough to promise an end to the insurgency. In fact, the government's spirit of reconciliation was still limited. The state-controlled media continued to refer to RENAMO members as "armed bandits," and in December 1988 President Chissano refused the idea of negotiations with RENAMO, explaining that "the people will not allow us to talk to the murderers."[29]

On September 16, 1988, Pope John Paul II arrived in Maputo for a pastoral visit. In his arrival statement the pope said, "The church recognizes it has a duty to promote legitimate aspirations for peace and justice; to be a sign of reconciliation and love against all forms of hate; to act, in its sphere, as a source of communion, against all forms of division; to promote a civilization of love, without any discrimination supposedly based on political, philosophical, or religious convictions, on degrees of wealth or power, on color or race." He laid down a challenge to choose the path of peace, and he promised that the church would work for peace and development in Mozambique.[30]

At the time President Chissano was trying to put relations with South Africa back on track. The first tangible consequence was an agreement signed by Portugal, Mozambique, and South Africa in April 1988 to provide for the repair of the electrical transmission line from the Cabora Bassa Dam in Mozambique to South Africa. In September 1988 Chissano and President P. W. Botha met at Songo, the site of Cabora Bassa. Meetings on subjects such as migrant workers and transportation followed at the technical level. Chissano later continued this dialogue by meeting with F. W. de Klerk in July 1989, shortly before de Klerk replaced Botha as president of South Africa.

At the end of 1988 there were signs that the Cold War was ending in southern Africa. The hope for reconciliation was rewarded by the agreement—brokered by Assistant Secretary of State Crocker with support from Soviet diplomats—to begin implementation of the UN plan for Namibia's transition to independence. Angola and Cuba signed an agreement providing a timetable for the orderly, monitored departure of Cuban forces from Angola. There was now one less justification for the war between FRELIMO and RENAMO.

In this conflict the FRELIMO government and the RENAMO insurgency were the protagonist and antagonist. These two central players would have to cooperate for any process of dialogue and reconciliation to succeed. First, however, each side would have to develop its own peace option.

The situation seemed ripe for change. The stalemate in the war satisfied no one: The FAM's poor combat effectiveness was not improving; RENAMO operated at will throughout most of the countryside, but it held no provincial centers; the transport corridors that Zimbabwe depended on were not secure; and there were more than two million refugees, many in Malawi. The international environment had improved, and the government's domestic policies were becoming more pragmatic. However, FRELIMO still insisted that Mozambique remain a one-party state and contemplated reconciliation only on its own terms. The government strictly circumscribed political rights. RENAMO had yet to articulate any political program. Everyone needed an alternative to war.

FRELIMO would have to abandon Marxist-Leninist ideology and drop its insistence that Mozambique be a one-party state. The government would have to concede RENAMO a legitimate existence within the political system. To get across the message that the government now wanted to talk with RENAMO, President Chissano would have to declare publicly that FRELIMO policy had changed and develop confidential channels of communication to RENAMO to reinforce that message.

Dhlakama likewise had to create a peace option for RENAMO, and his task would be at least as hard. He would have to build a civilian party structure parallel to RENAMO's military organization. He would have to articulate a political program that demonstrated a willingness and readiness to negotiate. Like Chissano, Dhlakama would have to affirm that both FRELIMO and RENAMO could have important roles in the future Mozambique. He would have to build support within RENAMO for peace talks. Finally, he would have to use every available channel to signal RENAMO's desire for dialogue and peace.

Once both parties had developed peace options, they would have to create a formula for dialogue. RENAMO demanded that the two sides meet as equals, but the government insisted on its position as the sole legitimate force in Mozambique, as confirmed by its diplomatic status. International and regional connections to the conflict were changing. The Cold War was finally over, and U.S.-Soviet rivalry was no longer fueling regional conflicts. States in the region, especially South Africa and Zimbabwe, were beginning to look for ways to encourage detente in the region and to see their interests in terms of a peaceful Mozambique, with refugees returning home and the regional transport infrastructure secure.

Could other states help to develop the formula for dialogue? In the world of diplomacy outside states frequently intervene in a conflict or a negotiating process to protect or promote their own interests. As the pope had done, they could legitimize and give credibility to peace initiatives through public encouragement; those governments that had contact with RENAMO could offer a private channel for communication. They might offer the facilities and logistic support needed to convene a meeting of the two sides. Once negotiations got under way, there would be opportunities to help the peace process in other ways, and one government or the United Nations might take a leading position, perhaps as mediator.

two

Starting a Dialogue

Traditional diplomacy assumes a world of sovereign and equal states. But today many conflicts involve states, or entities trying to become recognized as states, that lack the full measure of legitimacy, capacity, or stability to function as sovereign states. The governments in these states may not control all the claimed national territory; they may be opposed by ethnic minorities claiming a right to self-determination and their own state; in trying to exert control over the population, these governments may violate human rights. This incapacity to perform the responsibilities of sovereignty can be seen in Africa, in the Balkans, in the polities emerging from the former Soviet Union, and elsewhere.

Diplomatic doctrine, geared to manage the conflicts that arise between states, denies nonstate actors any recognized role. This doctrine, which is embodied in the structure of the United Nations, does not provide adequate means for dealing with conflicts that involve parties not recognized as states. Perhaps the time has come to try more flexible approaches.

The most difficult moment in a dialogue aimed at ending a conflict can be the apparently simple act of convening talks. Starting out is difficult precisely because it raises this question of enormous importance: What degree of status do the parties stand to gain or lose by sitting at the same table? This fundamental question often cannot be answered to mutual satisfaction by the parties themselves. If they cannot find the right formula for opening a dialogue, perhaps a third party can help.

Third-party involvement can be either unobtrusive or high profile. *Good offices* signifies carrying out specific requests, such as presenting one side's message to the other. *Facilitation* implies a continuing role in organizing and sustaining a dialogue. *Mediation* means managing the dialogue, with the power to influence the agenda and format for the talks and to formulate proposals for discussion. *Arbitration* requires an agreement from the parties to grant the third party the power to put forward terms for settlement. Third-party involvement normally starts out as good offices, and it may grow into facilitation or mediation. Arbitration is rare.

The good officer, facilitator, or mediator is a go-between who works for reconciliation: to reunite the parties in a more harmonious relationship. Unlike a mediator in the commercial environment, who can work to resolve one dispute in relative isolation, a mediator in diplomacy must both resolve a dispute and construct a new relationship between the parties. This aspect of mediation is even more significant when the conflict involves parties competing for power within a single state.

The involvement of a third party in the negotiating process always adds complications. The parties must trust the mediator, who must be neutral or whose biases must be evident from the outset. Mediators must be creative and precise, able to express the concerns of the parties in non-prejudicial language. They need patience and determination to move a long, painstaking process past the inevitable barriers and setbacks. Mediation is not an easy job.

To get a dialogue started, a third party can identify which parties need to be included in the talks, work out a common understanding of the initial rules of engagement, arrange for the parties to come to the table, provide a site for the talks, and establish a constructive ambiance. Even when third parties can help launch negotiations, they rarely have the power to convoke the parties. Former colonial rulers, great powers, neighboring states, regional organizations, and the United Nations have all played this role.

Moving toward Talks: 1989 to June 1990

By the end of 1988 both sides were rethinking their options and exploring how to promote their interests by dialogue, not war.

In the summer of 1988 Dhlakama met in Germany with Kenya's foreign minister. Over the next two years Bethuel Kiplagat, permanent secretary of Kenya's Foreign Ministry, was to have numerous meetings with RENAMO officials and to arrange passports, travel, and overseas expenses for them.

In October 1988 President Daniel arap Moi of Kenya invited Presidents Chissano and Mugabe to meet in Nairobi to explore the possibilities for talks. Moi followed up in December by sending an envoy to meet with Dhlakama in Gorongosa.[1]

At a meeting in Maputo on February 9, 1989, South African Foreign Minister Roelof "Pik" Botha suggested to Chissano that Mozambique ask the United States to mediate an end to the war. Chissano responded that the United States should not try to become a mediator but that a "constructive role" by it or some other government would be welcome.[2]

Mozambican church leaders launched a second track for exploring contacts. First, Cardinal Alexander dos Santos, Archbishop Don Jaime Goncalves, Anglican Bishop Dinis Sengulane, and Pastor Jeremias Mucache (president of the Christian Council of Mozambique) met with Chissano to urge that he begin a dialogue with RENAMO. He agreed that the church leaders should meet outside Mozambique with RENAMO representatives, but their first contacts with RENAMO's external wing yielded no tangible results. In February 1989 in Nairobi the church leaders met RENAMO's internal leaders. They asked both the government and RENAMO to commit to the principle of renouncing violence as a way to bring about change; although far from a concrete agreement on a cease-fire, this principle could be the basis for a dialogue.

On April 7, 1989, RENAMO sent telexes to the pope and to the Community of Sant'Egidio referring to a unilateral RENAMO cease-fire in Nampula Province and asking both to urge the FAM to respect the cease-fire.[3] Sant'Egidio, after checking with Italian government officials, invited Dhlakama to come to Rome on an unofficial visit. On May 2 RENAMO sent another message to the Holy See from its headquarters in Gorongosa. After warning that FRELIMO's recent steps to improve the situation of the Catholic Church in Mozambique were not sincere, the two-page letter recalled the confiscation of ecclesiastical property and the desanctification of many churches. The letter explained that, unlike the FRELIMO leadership, "many of us, combatants from both the political and military cadres of RENAMO, including our President, are Catholics."

Chissano wanted direct talks between the parties to be arranged as an internal matter between the legitimate government and a dissident organization. He prepared a twelve-point plan and asked the church leaders to use their good offices to present it to RENAMO at a meeting in Nairobi on July 12. A FAM-Zimbabwean offensive against RENAMO in central Mozambique caused this meeting to be postponed.

On July 17, 1989, President Chissano told a news conference in Maputo that the church leaders and a government delegation had been prepared to meet with a RENAMO delegation but that the insurgents had not appeared for the meeting. He said the government's twelve-point paper called on RENAMO to renounce violence, but he did not go into details.

Meanwhile, Chissano engaged in a series of international contacts designed to bolster his position before an upcoming FRELIMO party congress. Several days earlier U.S. Assistant Secretary of State Herman J. Cohen had announced in Maputo that the United States accepted Chissano's request for help in ending the war. Presidents Moi and Mugabe, who were the next visitors to Maputo, announced support for the peace process, giving Chissano's efforts a psychological lift before the opening of FRELIMO's fifth party congress. South Africa's F. W. de Klerk was due to visit the following week.[4] The idea of talking to RENAMO, previously anathema, was gaining currency.

At the end of July FRELIMO's fifth party congress debated whether to open talks with RENAMO. In his address, Zambia's President Kenneth Kaunda urged the congress to authorize the government to talk to RENAMO's leaders to "find out what they think they are doing to themselves and to their brothers and sisters, and on whose command they are doing it."[5] Chissano presented the case for negotiation and reconciliation: "We are going to reach into the minds of the RENAMO chiefs. We are going to save them from the clutches of those who control them."[6] Andrea Riccardi, who was invited to address the congress, offered Sant'Egidio's full support for a peace process in any place, near or far. According to Foreign Minister Pascoal M. Mocumbi, the congress decided that direct talks could begin with RENAMO, but first the insurgents had to renounce violence and accept constitutional rule.

From August 8 to 11 the church leaders met in Nairobi with a RENAMO delegation led by Dhlakama. The church leaders presented Chissano's twelve-point paper, which demanded that all groups renounce terrorism, banditry, and all forms of violence and which offered a commitment to reintegrate former insurgents into society and politics upon normalization of relations. Dhlakama presented a RENAMO paper for transmission to Chissano. The Kenyan Foreign Ministry announced that both sides agreed to continue meeting to work toward the goal of direct talks between FRELIMO and RENAMO. While Dhlakama was in Nairobi, he met with Edward Fugit, a U.S. diplomat who was then the charge d'affaires at the U.S. embassy in Harare.[7] The United States was already looking at the initial peace moves in the context of its overall regional strategy to reduce conflict throughout southern Africa.

On August 15 the church leaders presented to Chissano the sixteen-point position paper given to them by Dhlakama. This paper stated that

RENAMO did not intend to use armed struggle to change the existing order in Mozambique. It criticized the presence of foreign forces brought in by FRELIMO as an obstacle to peace and an infringement of Mozambique's sovereignty and independence, but it offered to take into consideration the interests of neighboring states in resolving the conflict. It affirmed that "the people are sovereign and have inalienable rights to elect their leader that will serve their expectations and their essential traditions." The paper's final point stated: "RENAMO wants a genuine negotiation conducive to national reconciliation without victors or vanquished, and without recrimination followed by constitutional reform; united efforts in order to form a new Mozambique where brotherhood will be affirmed by free debate of ideas and decision of consensus; a new Mozambique where armed struggle need never be the last and only resort for the solution of our problems."

The next day a brief Mozambican newspaper report noted simply that Presidents Moi and Mugabe were expected to report to President Chissano on the meeting in Nairobi.[8]

The papers given by both sides to the church leaders contained principles that could serve as the basis for dialogue. Both wanted a peaceful solution, a democracy based on freedom of expression and association, the right of all citizens to full participation in society, recognition that the people are sovereign and have the right to choose their government, and a peace process based on a desire for national reconciliation and unity. Both accepted the possibility of change through the democratic process, and RENAMO did not rule out accepting the legitimacy of the government, the constitution, and the laws in force.

On August 22, 1989, Dhlakama declared a moratorium on RENAMO attacks on the Nacala corridor. This announcement reportedly followed a deal involving the government of Malawi, which depended on the rail line in the Nacala corridor as its most direct route for exports, and the British-based corporation LONRHO.[9] LONRHO has extensive mining and agricultural investments throughout southern Africa. Roland "Tiny" Rowland, LONRHO's president, had in a long career earned a reputation for making things happen in Africa. At several points in the Mozambique peace process his personal involvement would be crucial.

When in September 1989 Chissano addressed the Non-Aligned Summit in Belgrade, he dismissed RENAMO's claim to be a legitimate opposition movement and retreated from the positions he had asked the church leaders to present to RENAMO. He rejected the idea of multiparty government in Mozambique on the ground that he would not accept any arrangement that undermined national unity or divided power.

Because of their different positions as a recognized government and an unrecognized insurgency, the two sides had contradicting perspectives on how to set up a dialogue. Chissano wanted to use the good offices of the church leaders to define a basis for direct talks. He wanted to avoid outside involvement along the lines of the Namibia negotiations, which were led by the United States and included massive UN involvement. If private citizens could not arrange the dialogue with RENAMO, he was willing to involve an African government, preferably Zimbabwe, because the government in Harare was an ally. Involvement by an African government, unlike involvement by a western government or the United Nations, would not seem to violate his insistence on absolute national sovereignty. RENAMO's perspectives were the opposite: It wanted a major, intrusive third-party role. If the mediator were to be African, it should be the Kenyan government. Lisbon, despite the colonial past, was acceptable, and eventually the United Nations should play a major role.

During the fall of 1989 both sides kept up their outside contacts. As for Dhlakama's possible unofficial visit to Rome, in June 1989 he had thanked Prime Minister Andreotti's chief of staff for the invitation but postponed traveling because of the military situation in Mozambique. In October the RENAMO delegation in Nairobi told Archbishop Goncalves, who had recently been in Rome for meetings with Vatican and Italian officials, that Dhlakama wanted to go to Rome to meet with both Goncalves and with Andreotti. In mid-November Chissano sent Teodato Hunguana (now minister of information) to meet with the Vatican's foreign minister, Archbishop Angelo Sodano. In early December both Guebuza and Dhlakama were in Nairobi to discuss the peace process with the Kenyan government.

From December 6 to 9 FRELIMO's central committee discussed potential changes to accommodate RENAMO's call for multiparty democracy. The answer was no. The concluding report stated that such a system could not be imposed by force, that it would intensify Mozambique's internal divisions, and that the people did not want it. As an alternative it suggested broadening popular participation in FRELIMO.

Three months later, during the second week of March 1990, Dhlakama came to Rome for meetings set up by Sant'Egidio. He met officials of the Italian Foreign Ministry but missed his appointment at the Vatican. He told members of Sant'Egidio that the war could not be won by either side and that he wanted to start a dialogue with the government. He spoke with Goncalves to explore the possibility of activating the Mozambican bishops as mediators who could help overcome the distrust between the two sides. Chissano had already opposed this option because he wanted any third-party role limited to good offices for setting up talks and because FRELIMO had a history of poor relations with religious authorities.

On March 12 President Chissano met President Bush in Washington. He told Bush that he was ready to enter into direct talks with RENAMO, without preconditions such as a previous cease-fire. At the departure ceremony Bush said Chissano had taken "significant steps to heal divisions which threaten your nation. . . . We urge all parties to talk at the earliest opportunity so as to avoid further suffering."[10]

On March 27 Mozambique's foreign minister, Pascoal Mocumbi, met the Vatican's Archbishop Sodano. Mocumbi confirmed that Chissano was working with Zimbabwe and Kenya to launch a dialogue, but he said that the Mozambican government would appreciate help from the Vatican to strengthen the peace process.

Holy See diplomacy has often provided good offices to open communication between parties to a conflict, but the Vatican has rarely taken on a higher profile role such as mediator. The nuncio in the capital concerned normally provides the good offices, but at times the national bishops' conference has taken the leading role. Only in exceptional circumstances would the Holy See provide a venue for a meeting between the parties.

In April, Chissano sent Minister of Labor Aguiar Mazula as his personal emissary to Rome for meetings set up outside normal diplomatic channels by Sant'Egidio. At the Vatican he met with Monsignor Jean-Louis Tauran, Sodano's deputy at the Foreign Ministry, and later with Cardinal Agostino Casaroli. Mazula said that President Chissano accepted the role being played by Kenya and Zimbabwe, but there was a difficulty in agreeing on a venue for the talks. Malawi was the most likely venue (preferred by the government), but RENAMO wanted to meet in Europe, most likely in Lisbon. Without mentioning Rome as a venue, Mazula raised the possibility that the Community of Sant'Egidio might be asked to provide support for direct talks. The Vatican did not object to this possibility but left it up to the parties to deal directly with Sant'Egidio.

On June 7 Maputo's semiofficial newspaper *Noticias* announced that RENAMO had agreed to begin direct peace talks in Malawi at a date soon to be announced. The newspaper carried an editorial entitled "Dialogue for the End of the War." The editorial reviewed Chissano's initiative to launch a peace process, including the statement he made during his visit to Washington in March that the government was ready to conduct direct talks with RENAMO.

On June 12 a RENAMO delegation led by Dhlakama and a government delegation led by Guebuza and Mocumbi arrived in Blantyre, Malawi.[11] Dhlakama arrived aboard a LONRHO corporate jet, accompanied by Tiny Rowland and Bethuel Kiplagat, the permanent secretary in Kenya's Foreign Ministry.[12] The next day the government of Malawi announced that the talks had been aborted: "Owing to apparent difficulties experienced by the RENAMO and Kenya delegations it was not possible to initiate the process of direct talks between the Mozambique Government delegation and RENAMO. . . . Efforts are continuing to set a new date in the near future for the process to begin in Malawi."[13]

Round One: July 8–10, 1990

After the aborted session in Malawi, Sant'Egidio's leaders moved quickly to convene talks in Rome. In mid-May they had already taken the occasion of a visit by Cardinal dos Santos and Archbishop Goncalves to Rome to develop the option of bringing the parties to Rome for exploratory talks, without any insistence that the issue of a mediator be addressed. Now they resumed contacts by telephone, and both sides indicated a willingness to meet in Rome. Sant'Egidio's headquarters could be a site for the meeting. Andrea Riccardi had secured promises of Italian government financial and diplomatic support from Prime Minister Giulio Andreotti and Foreign Minister Gianni de Michelis. To assist with the talks, they named Mario Raffaelli, a Socialist member of parliament who had worked with Andreotti at the Foreign Ministry, where for six years he had been under-secretary with special responsibility for Africa.

On June 16, just three days after the failure of talks in Malawi, Raul Domingos arrived in Rome to ask Sant'Egidio to host a meeting of the two sides and the Italian government to underwrite the costs. Within a week, on June 24, President Chissano told the Italian ambassador in Maputo that the government was ready to send a delegate to Rome to meet with RENAMO.[14]

The two Mozambican delegations met for the first time at Sant'Egidio on the afternoon of July 8, 1990. Armando Emilio Guebuza headed the government's delegation, which included Teodato Hunguana (minister of information), Aguiar Mazula (minister of labor), and Francisco Madeira (presidential diplomatic adviser). Raul Domingos, in charge of RENAMO's external affairs, was joined by Vicente Ululu (head of the Department of Information), Agostinho Murrial (from the Department of Political Affairs), and Joao Almirante (from Dhlakama's cabinet).

At this point the four persons present who had set up the meeting were termed "observers." Mario Raffaelli was joined by Don Jaime Goncalves, the archbishop of Beira and head of Mozambique's episcopal conference. Andrea Riccardi and Don Matteo Zuppi represented the Community of Sant'Egidio.

The meeting was held in Sant'Egidio's largest meeting room. Its windows front onto a cloistered garden, and four large Byzantine icons of saints hang on the facing wall. Its vaulted ceiling and walls are painted white, and the floor is tiled with brick. The two Mozambican delegations were ranged on opposite sides of a large, U-shaped table; the four observers sat at the bend in the U. Zuppi gave the floor first to Riccardi.

Professor Riccardi, recalling that the purpose of the meeting was to promote dialogue between Mozambicans, quoted Pope John XXIII's invitation to Vatican Council II: "Let us seek more that which unites than that which divides." That precept could provide useful guidance for the work ahead. Whatever the painful experiences of the past during the years of civil war, the challenge now was to move away from war toward a peaceful dialogue within the framework of Mozambican unity.

Raffaelli said recent international events had shown that conversation and dialogue were the only way to resolve conflicts. To conduct a successful dialogue, starting with this historic meeting, the parties should favor that which unites over that which divides, avoid recriminations about the past, and seek ways to express their differences peacefully within a framework of pluralism and national unity. A reasonable first goal would be to agree on how, where, and when to continue the dialogue. The Italian government would give political and economic support for the dialogue.

During the next hour, Guebuza and Domingos made opening statements to introduce the members of their delegations and to express a commitment to dialogue. Both avoided contentious remarks, and the atmosphere was good. After some discussion, Raffaelli summed up that both sides seemed to agree that Italy would be the site for future meetings and that joint communiques could be used to inform the press of the talks. The questions of finding a mediator and creating an agenda for the talks remained open. Guebuza and Domingos both said that the four observers should continue in that role at the peace talks.

Raffaelli presided over the meeting that began late the next morning and continued until mid-afternoon. Discussion of what kind of role might be played by a third party and which third party would be appropriate led immediately to an impasse. The Mozambican government had long insisted that talks between the two sides be direct, with any third-party role being minimal and designed to decrease in significance as the peace process went forward. The RENAMO delegation did not trust either the government's good faith or its own ability to hold the government to commitments made in direct, bilateral talks. Raul Domingos said that having a mediator present at all times could compensate for the lack of trust between the two sides.

Those present discussed several options for mediation. The governments of both Kenya and Zimbabwe had helped with the initial contacts between the two parties, suggesting that they might become a tandem team of mediators. RENAMO would accept no formal role for Zimbabwe, whose troops were then conducting a last major offensive against RENAMO, and the government would accept Kenya only if Zimbabwe had an equal role as mediator.

Could the two sides agree on an agenda? The government saw the overall peace process as beginning with a cease-fire, after which RENAMO members would be reintegrated into Mozambican society. The government insisted that its new constitution and plan for elections be accepted by RENAMO. RENAMO wanted agreement on changing the system, including the constitution, and irreversible steps to do so before any cease-fire. Then one unified national defense force would have to be created out of the FAM and RENAMO forces, after which multiparty elections should be held. The meeting adjourned for a late lunch.

When they met again in early evening, there was immediate deadlock over the question of asking the governments of Kenya and Zimbabwe to mediate. To sidestep that issue, both parties agreed that the peace process required witnesses and that the four observers should continue to play that role. As for an agenda, it could be a combination of proposals already made. The four observers then took the lead in working out that combination.

The next day was spent in drafting and negotiating a joint communique, with the observers facilitating the work by shuttling between the two delegations in their hotels until agreement was reached. In the communique, the two sides expressed satisfaction at their first direct, open, and frank talks; expressed interest in a constructive search for lasting peace, agreeing on the need to set aside sources of division and to seek mutual understanding; and committed themselves to search for ways to end the war and to create normal political, economic, and social conditions for all Mozambican citizens and to meet again in Rome at a time convenient for both. Privately, they had agreed to return to Rome in about two weeks. The communique was signed by Guebuza, Domingos, and the four observers. Raffaelli adjourned the meeting.

That night the Sant'Egidio hosts had reason to celebrate. Despite the deadlock on the issue of African mediators, the parties had agreed on a time and place to continue the dialogue. The atmosphere in the meetings had been good, with both sides avoiding recriminations and looking toward the future reconstruction of the country. Contacts with the Italian government had reassured Sant'Egidio of official support for the talks, including an essential commitment to cover the expenses involved in hosting the Mozambican delegations in Rome. Given the difficulties that had been overcome in convening the talks, even a partial success gave hope to the situation.

Raffaelli explained, in an interview on Radio Vatican, how the first round of direct talks had been convened. First, the governments of Kenya and Zimbabwe had narrowed the positions of the parties so that they were both ready to consider direct talks. Then, "the good offices of the Italian government, through myself, and of the Community of Sant'Egidio and thus the Church, produced this [first round of direct talks]."[15]

Riccardi and Zuppi, the two observers from Sant'Egidio, sent a note to Prime Minister Andreotti to report on the first meetings. They said a positive step had been taken, even if the questions of mediation and of the agenda were unresolved. They signaled a need for financial support to cover the costs of hosting the two delegations in Rome. Their memorandum reported that Assistant Secretary of State Cohen had met with them and promised U.S. encouragement and support for the peace process.[16]

Domingos traveled to Lisbon after the July round to meet with Portuguese government officials.

Round Two: August 11–14, 1990

On July 26 the government's delegation returned to Rome for the next round of talks. Domingos was meanwhile in Nairobi, where he spent the next two weeks. RENAMO's delegation depended on Kenya for travel documents, and they blamed this delay on the Kenyans. Most of the RENAMO delegation eventually arrived in Rome before Domingos, who stayed in Africa to meet again with Dhlakama. The Kenyans were persuading RENAMO to insist that the Kenyan government be asked to assume a direct role as sole mediator, a demand that the government would surely reject.

While RENAMO delayed, on the evening of July 31 President Chissano told the FRELIMO politburo that the situation was now ready for putting a multiparty system in place. Chissano was both offering to RENAMO the major reform it had demanded and signaling that RENAMO should engage in serious talks if it did not want to be left behind. In Rome the FRELIMO delegation met with Prime Minister Andreotti; RENAMO missed its meeting with Andreotti.

After Domingos arrived on August 10, the talks began with an informal series of discussions between the observers and each delegation at a retreat at Rocca di Pappa in the Alban Hills about fifteen miles south of Rome.

On Saturday, August 11, James Creagan, the charge d'affaires at the U.S. embassy to the Holy See, and Randall Lecocq, Mozambique desk officer for the Department of State, met with Domingos. This was the first U.S. contact with RENAMO in the context of the Rome peace talks. After Assistant Secretary Cohen's meeting at Sant'Egidio in July, the office of the State Department's spokesman had issued a statement welcoming the outcome of the first round of talks and commending both sides; when Creagan met with Domingos, he affirmed these points directly. Regarding the unresolved mediator issue, Creagan suggested this was a procedural question that could be postponed while discussion of substantive points began within the current negotiating framework. The important point was to move discussions toward a cease-fire.

Domingos was unmoved. He had returned to Rome to resolve one issue: securing a proper mediation. Kenya had helped RENAMO in its early international contacts and was still the only government willing to give RENAMO travel documents. Domingos would not agree to exclude Kenya. It would be absurd for RENAMO to agree to mediation by Zimbabwe, a combatant.

Domingos had other concerns. He wanted the United States to provide more technical expertise to support the talks. RENAMO trusted the four observers, but their experience in these matters was limited. The United States should adopt a more balanced stance vis-a-vis the parties. So far it had offered full support to the FRELIMO government, refused contacts with RENAMO, and published the Gersony report that was heavily critical of RENAMO. The party that had fought for democracy and multiparty elections in Mozambique was RENAMO, not FRELIMO. President Dhlakama should have an early meeting with Assistant Secretary Cohen. RENAMO's plan for the talks was to settle the mediator issue at this round, then to resolve all political issues, and only at the end of the negotiating process to discuss a cease-fire.

On August 12 Domingos asked to meet with Guebuza one on one. It was a chance for the two delegation leaders to exchange information on negotiating positions before the formal sessions. Guebuza, who eventually wanted to move the negotiating process into direct, bilateral talks without any active mediation, had an opportunity to try out ideas on his counterpart. Would RENAMO accept that Kenya's role might be "observer" rather than mediator, or alternatively that the negotiation continue under the auspices of Sant'Egidio? Domingos took the occasion to repeat RENAMO's positions: Kenya must have a role in the negotiations; the government must accept RENAMO's participation as a political party in Mozambique; foreign troops must be withdrawn from Mozambique; and a cease-fire would be possible only after agreement on a transitional period and under UN supervision.

On Monday, August 13, at Sant'Egidio's meeting hall Zuppi called a plenary session to order. Riccardi, in his welcoming remarks, emphasized again the need to develop, through the negotiations, a moral and political culture of dialogue and peace.

Raffaelli expressed the greetings of the Italian government and the satisfaction that despite difficulties the two sides had come together again to continue their dialogue. The Italian government and the European Economic Community had both issued extremely positive statements on the launching of the dialogue in July. The Italian Parliament had passed a resolution promising the government the means to support the peace process. Whatever difficulties the dialogue might encounter, a positive attitude would help the two parties overcome specific problems.

Guebuza, after thanking the Italian government for its hospitality, turned directly to the mediator question. His government would accept a joint Kenyan-Zimbabwean mediation or, if this was unacceptable, direct talks between the parties. In any case, the question of a mediator should not become an obstacle to talks between Mozambicans themselves. He then discussed briefly the steps decided on by FRELIMO's politburo to establish a multiparty system in Mozambique.

Domingos said RENAMO had come to negotiate toward a new, democratic future for the country. As to the steps taken by the government, they were unilateral and did not include all Mozambicans. RENAMO was concerned that the government might not reflect in its actions at home the attitudes its delegation expressed in the peace talks—at home the government media still called RENAMO "armed bandits." As for the work of this round, the key point was to agree on the question of a mediator.

In the discussion that followed, Guebuza played down the question of a mediator and invited Domingos to discuss other issues. Domingos refused, insisting on a central role for Kenya, although RENAMO might consider this role being described as "observer" or "facilitator." Guebuza said he would think it over.

Domingos brought up the issue of foreign troops in Mozambique, especially those from Zimbabwe, which he accused of participating directly in the Mozambican civil war on the side of the government. Guebuza parried, insisting that such problems could be discussed only in the ambit of an agreed agenda. Domingos was unmoved and replied that the government should look at this issue from the perspective of those who were suffering from the presence of foreign troops.

Raffaelli, in closing the session, said that the moment was delicate for the peace process. The two immediate challenges were to establish a framework for the next meetings (i.e. the mediator issue) and to find a way to emphasize the responsibility of both sides to avoid taking steps that might compromise their dialogue. Both sides accepted Zuppi's proposal that the next round of talks be held between September 10 and 18 in Rome.

Because RENAMO insisted on resolving the mediator issue—or rather Kenya's role—first, the talks stopped here. Both sides, however, had shown some flexibility: The government was willing to consider a specific role for Kenya, even if not the position of sole mediator; RENAMO was willing to consider falling back to giving Kenya a role as observer or guarantor of an eventual agreement. No doubt there was disappointment among the government delegation that after waiting two weeks in Rome for RENAMO, they were unable to discuss anything beyond procedural questions. RENAMO had gained the satisfaction of seeing that its views had to be taken into account. The four observers had the satisfaction of confirming that both sides wanted to go on with the talks, but they needed to find a formula for getting beyond the mediator issue.

On August 14 a brief formal session at Sant'Egidio registered agreement on a joint communique. This time the text emphasized that the parties remained determined to continue their dialogue. The current meetings had included a "direct and frank dialogue." The parties agreed that they should suspend the meetings to examine some complex issues and should resume meetings in Rome shortly.[17] The communique gave no date for the next meeting.

When Prime Minister Andreotti briefly met with the RENAMO delegation the same day, he advised Domingos that it might not be possible, given the government's position, to reach agreement that Kenya would become mediator.

In the time before the next round it was expected that the parties would consult at home on options for resolving the mediator issue. Although both sides had been willing to listen to alternative solutions, neither delegation had the authority from headquarters to conclude a deal not envisaged in their opening positions. As for the possibility of an Italian mediation, the government of Italy, while willing enough to support the talks or be present as observer or facilitator, demonstrated no desire to play an active role as mediator. One possible way forward was to let the issue slide, allowing the four observers who were already facilitating the talks to play the role of mediators without any formal title. The observers from Sant'Egidio planned to meet with Dhlakama in early September to urge him to accept another role for Kenya, perhaps as guarantor of any cease-fire agreement.

To prepare for this meeting, Sant'Egidio's two observers sent Dhlakama a memorandum sketching out several possible solutions. Among these was the alternative later to be adopted: The four observers would collectively take on the role of mediator, Sant'Egidio and the Italian government would provide hospitality and logistic support, Kenya could advise RENAMO delegates, and a committee of other governments and the United Nations could be formed to guarantee implementation of any peace agreement.

Before Domingos left Rome, he met with representatives of the International Committee of the Red Cross (ICRC). They wanted to discuss a proposal the ICRC had prepared in June to create non-combat zones and corridors for delivery of humanitarian supplies, with the goal of lessening the flow of refugees out of the country. This proposal called for each side to issue a unilateral statement that hostilities had been suspended in the areas specified and that there would be no attacks against those areas or from those areas. This arrangement would permit the civilian population to return, at least for the agricultural cycle from October to May. In general the government looked with favor on an extension of ICRC activities.

Domingos simply listened. RENAMO considered the ICRC proposal with suspicion. RENAMO leaders feared that the government could use any lull in the fighting to plan new attacks on RENAMO units, and they realized that a series of noncombat zones would inevitably deprive RENAMO units of mobility, making them more vulnerable to attack. Moreover, any commitment to limit fighting would reduce RENAMO's one instrument of pressure on the government.

After leaving Rome, Domingos went to Lisbon for more talks with Portuguese authorities.

Riccardi and Zuppi traveled to Africa at the end of August to resolve the mediator issue. In Nairobi they met for the first time with Permanent Secretary Kiplagat; the two sides had a chance to discuss their separate roles, minimize mutual suspicions, and agree on the need to convince the parties to engage seriously in negotiations. Kiplagat said that in the early stages of negotiations Kenya could accept a role as facilitator, on the understanding that Kenya could have a more direct role in implementing and guaranteeing any peace agreement.

Riccardi and Zuppi planned to meet Dhlakama in Nairobi to discuss the mediator issue. The meeting with Dhlakama never took place. Domingos, who did show up for a meeting in Malawi, explained that a major offensive by the FAM, allegedly supported by Zimbabwe, was under way near Milange in Zambezia Province and that Dhlakama had to remain in Gorongosa to direct the RENAMO defensive. He said RENAMO needed secure communications between Dhlakama's headquarters in Gorongosa and the delegation in Rome (a request made repeatedly but never fully satisfied). Domingos agreed to think over the suggestion that the mediator issue might be resolved by asking the observers to play this role, and he promised that the RENAMO delegation would return to Rome.

When Riccardi and Zuppi went to Maputo, Chissano told them that he would accept no role for Kenya either at the table or in the room where negotiations were taking place. Chissano readily agreed that the observers should be promoted to the position of mediators.

On September 15, when the next round of negotiations was expected to begin, Assistant Secretary Cohen came to Rome to meet with both sides and the four observers. Cohen wanted to hear the views of all, to encourage a solution to the mediator issue, to offer U.S. facilitation and technical advice, to promote early involvement of military commanders in talks aimed at a cease-fire, and to urge both sides to cooperate with the ICRC in expediting the delivery of humanitarian assistance. This would be Cohen's first meeting with Domingos.

Neither side sent its full negotiating team to Rome.[18] In response to a FAM offensive in the Milange District, RENAMO issued from Gorongosa a communique demanding the withdrawal of all Zimbabwean troops from Mozambique as a condition for peace talks. Cohen met separately with Mazula and Domingos. He sketched out the role the United States intended to play—supporting the current negotiating framework by offering facilitation and expert advice. He urged them to resolve the mediator issue. Cohen assured the observers that the United States would support their efforts.

Raffaelli and the other observers met separately with Mazula and Domingos. The observers thought that the Kenyan role could be removed as a stumbling block in the second half of October, when both sides expected to return to Rome to resume talks. They wanted the next round of talks to focus on a proposal to concentrate the Zimbabwean troops in the transport corridors and for both sides to pledge no attacks against the corridors or from the corridors. This proposal could serve the interests of all: Zimbabwe and the government would benefit from increased security for the transport corridors, and RENAMO would benefit from the restriction of Zimbabwean forces to the corridors. By separating the international aspects of the conflict from the internal problems, this proposal could simplify the challenge of organizing the dialogue between the parties.

Without commenting on the reasons for the abortion of the September round, the observers gave both sides a letter recalling the commitment to resume talks in September and the communication from RENAMO that it could not participate in talks because of a major FAM offensive. The letter expressed the view that talks should be resumed and that if they did not resume by the start of November, the observers might feel obliged to make a public statement ascribing responsibility for the failure to negotiate.

In an effort to confirm agreement on the mediator issue and to explain Sant'Egidio's proposal for the transport corridors, Raffaelli, Goncalves, and Zuppi traveled again to the region. On October 24 Dhlakama told them at a meeting in Nairobi that RENAMO would return to the negotiations in Rome at the beginning of November. He ratified the arrangement for the observers to be named mediators. He agreed to consider a proposed agenda that would start with negotiations to confine Zimbabwean troops to the transport corridors in conjunction with a cease-fire in those areas.

At a subsequent meeting in Maputo, President Chissano confirmed his approval of the promotion of the team of observers to become mediators. He said time might be running out for RENAMO. The assembly would soon approve the new constitution. Adoption of a political party law and an election law could follow shortly, with multiparty elections as soon as October 1991. Chissano told Raffaelli, Goncalves, and Zuppi that the Rome talks should move forward to keep pace with domestic reform.[19] He agreed that the negotiations could resume with discussions of the presence of Zimbabwean troops and the security of the transport corridors. He took on the responsibility of explaining this decision to the Zimbabwean government.

Round Three: November 9 to December 1, 1990

In response to requests that the United States support the negotiations, the Department of State sent to the third round of talks a delegation headed by Robert Perito, the director of southern African affairs. Shortly after arrival, Perito met with Domingos, who said RENAMO was now ready to promote the four observers to the role of mediator. Domingos insisted that the first substantive item on the agenda be the withdrawal of Zimbabwean troops; discussion of the political system, multi-party elections, and establishment of a unified national army could follow in that order.

Perito met twice with government negotiator Guebuza. The U.S. team, which included Lieutenant Colonel Charles Snyder (military adviser in the Bureau of African Affairs) and other experts who were participating in the negotiations to end Angola's civil war, described possible cease-fire arrangements and options for organizing elections. Guebuza insisted that, whatever the involvement of the international community in implementing an agreement, the government would permit nothing that would appear to infringe on Mozambique's sovereignty.

The mediators worried about whether RENAMO's delegation was ready and able to perform in a complex negotiation. Domingos's habit of adamantly asserting his requirements and then rejecting other proposals suggested that Dhlakama had not given the delegation the authority to explore alternatives. The poor communication between Rome and RENAMO headquarters in Gorongosa aggravated the consequences of this restricted delegation of authority. The mediators were also concerned that Kenya's Bethuel Kiplagat, who intended to accompany Dhlakama to Rome and coach RENAMO's delegation from the sidelines, might be a complicating influence on the RENAMO leader.

Although the need for humanitarian relief supplies put increasing pressure on both sides, neither introduced this subject in the Rome negotiations. Nevertheless, this problem was a constant, important part of the dealings both had with the international community. On November 8 in Geneva, Dhlakama met with officials of the ICRC, including its president, Cornelio Sommaruga. Dhlakama told Sommaruga that RENAMO would like to permit properly identified ICRC vehicles and staff to circulate in specified areas, but in fact he promised only that RENAMO would examine specific requests that the ICRC might later make.

Perito met with Dhlakama after the RENAMO leader arrived in Rome on November 9. Dhlakama said he wanted to go ahead with the peace talks and would not be thrown off course by a FAM offensive then taking place. He told Perito that the United States should support the talks and give help to RENAMO, including expert advice on the issues being negotiated, a secure communication link (preferably by satellite) between

Rome and RENAMO headquarters in Gorongosa, and a more powerful transmitter for RENAMO's radio station. Dhlakama wanted a meeting with Assistant Secretary Cohen. The U.S. team made a presentation on cease-fire provisions and options for elections, explaining the arrangements under consideration by the Angolan parties. Dhlakama told Perito that he could not stay in Rome to direct the RENAMO delegation for more than a few days, because his presence was required in Mozambique.

On the evening of November 9, the first plenary session of the third round was held. Raffaelli and Riccardi spoke briefly to welcome the returning delegations. They suggested that circumstances were favorable for the resumption of talks and hoped that the negotiations would continue until peace was reached. Then Guebuza affirmed that the government's delegation wanted to discuss all issues in depth and without interruption.

Domingos, after expressing confidence that peace could be reached through dialogue, said two issues had to be addressed first: the structure of the mediation and the presence of Zimbabwean troops. Domingos proposed that the four observers become the mediators, with support from the Italian government. Guebuza accepted this proposal and agreed that the question of Zimbabwean troops could be first on the agenda. Raffaelli summed up: At the request of the parties the observers would agree to become mediators, and they would work up a proposal for an agenda, with the issue of Zimbabwean troops as the first item.[20]

The next afternoon, November 10, the parties accepted this agenda proposed by the mediators:

1. Presence and role of the Zimbabwean military forces during the period prior to the proclamation of the cease-fire.
2. The creation of the political and military conditions for peace in the country.
   a) Calendar preparation and procedures for an election. Internal guarantees and international role in the electoral process.
   b) Calendar and procedures for the proclamation and the conduct of the cease-fire. Internal guarantees and international role in the implementation of the miliary agreements of the armed forces.

For the next few days the mediators consulted each party on the issue of Zimbabwean troops. Short of full withdrawal of all such troops, RENAMO was willing to look at the idea of confining them to the Beira corridor; the government insisted on allowing Zimbabwean troops to remain in the Limpopo corridor as well. Dhlakama was still in Rome. On November 13, at a second plenary session, the mediators presented a draft proposal that would concentrate Zimbabwean troops in the Beira and

Limpopo corridors, preliminary to withdrawal within three months. There would be a joint commission to verify compliance, and RENAMO would promise not to attack in the areas of the corridors. The mediators saw work on this issue as a way to build confidence in the negotiations.

Shortly after he arrived in Rome on November 14, Assistant Secretary Cohen met with Dhlakama. Cohen encouraged Dhlakama to seek a negotiated settlement, explaining that agreement on the mediators' proposal on the corridors could be an important step in the negotiating process. Agreement would boost RENAMO's stature. Dhlakama, showing a tendency that would reappear later in the negotiating process, eventually agreed with his interlocutor: RENAMO would try to work out a two-corridor arrangement. Dhlakama asked that the United States adopt a new attitude toward RENAMO to counter the negative impact of the Gersony report and that the United States help to move the negotiations forward.

In a meeting with the mediators Dhlakama raised the issue of guarantees for himself and RENAMO. In this context "guarantees" at times meant assurances of physical security once RENAMO had laid down its arms, but it always meant the availability of resources to pay for the entry of RENAMO's cadres into the money economy. Without such compensation, Dhlakama explained, he would seem to be getting nothing for his supporters while offering FRELIMO the benefits of peace.

The next morning, November 15, Cohen met with Guebuza. Cohen said the United States supported the mediators and their proposal on the transport corridors. The United States wanted to facilitate progress in the talks. Guebuza said the government also looked with favor on an ICRC proposal to open humanitarian corridors to distribute aid to refugees and displaced persons, including opening routes for delivery of food from staging areas in Malawi. As for delivery into RENAMO-controlled areas, Guebuza emphasized that considerations of national sovereignty would, of course, require that a control commission with government members be put in place to supervise the work of international agencies.

By the afternoon of November 15 the mediators had a written proposal before the parties. Its terms required that Zimbabwean troops be concentrated into the Beira and Limpopo corridors, each twenty kilometers (twelve miles) wide; RENAMO would promise not to attack the corridors; and a joint commission would be set up to supervise. The commission would have representatives from the two parties, from Zimbabwe, and from the Italian government. The mediators met with the delegations separately during the next two days. RENAMO came around to the idea of two corridors but insisted that they be much narrower than twenty kilometers. RENAMO wanted to work out all details before signing and to expand the membership of the commission to include Kenya, the United States, and Zambia.

There were no plenary meetings the week of November 19, during which the mediators kept going back and forth between the delegations to work out a deal. RENAMO now accepted a corridor that would include at most a strip of land extending only three kilometers (about two miles) from either side of the highway, railroad, and pipelines. The government, which agreed that Zimbabwean troops must be confined to the corridors, rejected any commitment that these troops should withdraw from Mozambique. The government balked at the mediators' proposal that there should be no military use of the corridors, explaining that such a limitation would be an unacceptable infringement of sovereignty. Alternatively, the mediators proposed that the text should bar offensive military use of the corridors, but the two parties had such different views of what should be considered "offensive military use" that there was no possibility of agreement on this basis. The parties had still not settled on the composition of the commission; RENAMO's request for additional members had been placed on the agenda, and the government indicated it might ask to include the United States and the Soviet Union.

On November 22 Guebuza and Francisco Madeira (President Chissano's diplomatic adviser) met with Domingos and Vicente Ululu. Both sides now accepted that the corridors should include a three-kilometer zone on either side of the transport lines. The remaining issue was military use of the corridors. The government, again insisting that there be no infringement of Mozambican sovereignty, rejected any restriction on its own use of national territory. RENAMO, which recalled that FAM and Zimbabwean troops repeatedly used the Beira corridor as a staging area for attacks against RENAMO, wanted practical assurances on how use of the corridor might be controlled.

The mediators consulted frequently with the U.S. team on the progress of the negotiations. To work out a deal between the parties on the issue of military use of the corridors, the mediators shuttled between the two delegations. The U.S. team, operating in parallel with the mediators in its own meetings with both parties, urged them to sign an agreement without a provision on military use of the corridors and to send this issue to the proposed control commission as one of its first items of business. The U.S. team advised RENAMO to put aside its insistence on settling all details first and to sign soon in order to capture the gains represented by the government's commitments to concentrate Zimbabwean troops in the corridors and to continue in a peace process aimed at multiparty elections. They urged the government delegation to sign an accord that would keep transport corridors open and get a peace process under way. At the end of November U.S. military experts briefed Domingos on cease-fire arrangements elsewhere and explained the practical difficulties in insisting on "no military use" of the corridors.

On the morning of November 30 the two parties and the mediators held a crucial plenary meeting at Sant'Egidio. In a paragraph-by-paragraph review of the text now proposed by the mediators, the two parties agreed on most points: RENAMO would nominate as members of the Joint Verification Commission (JVC) Kenya, Portugal, the United States, and Zambia; the government would nominate Congo, France, the Soviet Union, and the United Kingdom. The initial duration of the agreement would be extended from four to six months. Guebuza made a statement giving assurances that the government did not intend to use the corridors either to support a military escalation or to conduct offensive military operations. He agreed that this assurance could be transcribed in a side letter.

At another plenary meeting on the morning of December 1, the parties reviewed again the mediators' text for an agreement on the "presence and role of Zimbabwe's armed forces in the period prior to proclamation of the cease-fire." The two sides then signed. The mediators indicated they would make arrangements to host the first meeting of the JVC in Rome within two weeks so that it could organize its work.

Before leaving Rome the U.S. team met again with the mediators and with experts from the Italian Ministry of Defense. The mediators wanted to begin meetings with the parties as soon as possible on the item in the November 10 agenda regarding political issues, but first they thought it was necessary to sound out RENAMO on its goals. In addition, they had yet to satisfy RENAMO's desire for secure communication from Rome via Malawi to Gorongosa, a problem that made it difficult for the RENAMO delegation to consult with headquarters to revise RENAMO's often inflexible negotiating positions. The Italians had already prepared a basic document to set up the organization and procedures for the JVC.

Among the mediators, Goncalves must have felt a special sense of personal satisfaction at this agreement for a partial cease-fire. First of all, he was a Mozambican. Second, he had been the key link in developing the ties that led to the Italian mediation. His friendship with members of Sant'Egidio went back twenty years, and they had put him in contact with Italian political leaders, including Enrico Berlinguer. Goncalves had first discussed the peace process with Giulio Andreotti in 1988, when Andreotti was foreign minister; Andreotti was now prime minister and still a supporter of the peace negotiations. The Italian government's financial and logistic support would be essential for implementing the December 1 agreement and continuing the peace process.

Domingos stayed on in Rome for personal reasons. Before departing he asked for U.S. help and advice on political issues on the agenda. RENAMO would have to formulate and articulate views on a political party law and on an election system. The U.S. representative received this request favorably and urged RENAMO to prepare to act as a political party and to consider opening an office in Maputo. Domingos planned to leave Rome on December 14 to travel to Kenya for consultations with Dhlakama.

Round Three Continued: December 19–21, 1990

The remainder of the third round concentrated on two separate items: establishing the JVC and starting talks on political issues. Both parties had already responded favorably to the mediators' idea of a Christmas truce. The mediators wanted the parties to review a draft political agenda before Christmas, with talks set to resume in mid-January. The government negotiators hoped that the agenda would be coupled to a timetable for reaching agreement on the various points, and they intended to ask JVC members to provide financial resources to ease the government's burden of arranging logistic support for the JVC.

Because the RENAMO delegation was delayed in its return to Rome, the opening ceremonies for the JVC were postponed to December 19.

At its first meeting the JVC selected the Italian ambassador in Maputo, Manfredo Incisa di Camerana, as chairman. The JVC quickly decided that it would operate from Maputo and that its work would be supported by a Military Verification Committee, which would maintain monitoring teams at Beira and Chimoio in the Beira corridor and at Chokwe in the Limpopo corridor. The military committee would monitor military activities in the areas of the corridors, investigate incidents, maintain liaison with commanders, and report to the JVC.

On December 20 the JVC held a long, inconclusive session. There was no agreement on a precise definition of the two corridors. In limiting the corridors to strips three kilometers on either side of the transport lines, significant infrastructure (power lines, water sources, and the Chimoio airport) had been excluded. The government's representative and most members argued that for practical reasons these areas should be included in the corridors. The RENAMO representatives, none of whom had any experience in such meetings, refused to be drawn out and insisted on referring all questions to higher authorities. With only an agreement to meet in Maputo on December 27, the session adjourned.

When RENAMO's negotiators were under pressure to deal with the issues but unprepared to do so, their positions became rigid. On military matters RENAMO's delegation expressed appreciation for the advice from the U.S. military experts, and the RENAMO delegation seemed comfortable in discussion of military issues. Domingos described RENAMO's agreement with Malawi to keep the Nacala corridor open and explained that RENAMO had kept its word. But on the issue of international monitoring and verification, lack of political preparation and experience was affecting the negotiations.

It was even more difficult to engage RENAMO in discussion of political issues. Domingos rejected any timetable for resolving political issues. He was unmoved by the risk that the government would go forward with its own political reforms outside the context of the Rome talks. He insisted that political issues had to be dealt with serially, with the law on political parties coming first, then the election system, formation of a national army, and finally a cease-fire. If the Parliament in Maputo adopted any law on these issues before all of them had been discussed and agreed on in the context of the Rome talks, that law would simply be invalid. The December 21 communique that marked the end of this round of talks merely listed a series of fundamental principles, such as freedom of association, that should guide the discussion of political issues.

On December 27 and 31 the JVC met in Maputo to establish a precise and workable definition of the corridors. RENAMO began to express concerns about its own use of the corridors—after all, RENAMO forces would need on occasion to cross through the corridors, and the original agreement had been silent on this point. No conclusion was reached on the definition of the corridors and the military activity to be permitted in them. Perhaps the most significant point to emerge from the meetings was that, although the JVC had an independent basis for its activities in the December 1 agreement, both parties and all JVC members expected the JVC to be subordinate to the Rome negotiating process. This subordination served the Mozambican parties' interests: As long as the JVC was subordinate to the Rome process, its decisions would be subject to review by the two negotiating teams.

During the last six months of 1990 real progress had been made in starting a dialogue between the government and RENAMO.

The Sant'Egidio initiative had built on the results of the good offices performed by the four church leaders and by African governments, especially Kenya, Malawi, and Zimbabwe. Perhaps because Sant'Egidio was not a state, it could provide a venue and arrangements for talks in a way that avoided the question of the parties' status. In the first meeting, Sant'Egidio secured agreement to the two basic rules for the dialogue: that both sides would forswear the use of force as a means of securing their political goals and that they would emphasize that which unites rather than that which divides.

The second significant step in the negotiating process was the decision to name the four observers who had facilitated the first two rounds of talks as mediators. This step was a compromise between the government's desire for direct talks and RENAMO's insistence on an active role for the Kenyan government. Shortly after the mediators became responsible for managing the process of negotiation, they secured agreement on an initial agenda that included the issue of Zimbabwean forces, political issues, and a cease-fire. It remained to be seen how much authority to organize the peace process the parties were actually willing to delegate to the mediators.

Third, the December 1 agreement was an important step in separating the interests of neighboring states from the conflict among Mozambicans. Commercial movement through the corridors should no longer be threatened by war. This agreement thus simplified the military situation, and by establishing the JVC it created a structure through which outside governments could work to end Mozambique's war. However, it had thereby created a mechanism that could build or destroy confidence between the government and RENAMO. How well would these arrangements work in practice?

There were two major shortcomings. Nothing had been done to alleviate the suffering of the Mozambican people, through either a cease-fire or an agreement to expedite the work of humanitarian relief agencies. Nor had the parties committed themselves to any sense of urgency in the negotiating process.

three

Ordering the Peace Process

A mediator is responsible for managing the peace process. This responsibility requires giving order to three separate but eventually converging timelines:

- *The order in which issues are discussed*. Discussion involves both defining the issues and exploring various options for solution. Should issues be considered individually or grouped together? In theory a negotiator can maximize results for both sides by keeping the search for solutions separate from the advocacy of or commitment to specific solutions. In practice such separation is never easy and at times impossible.
- *The order in which commitments are made*. Every commitment made affects the context for making choices on remaining issues. It is common for negotiators to make easy commitments first, constructing the framework for an agreement while either leaving blanks for the difficult issues or putting brackets around alternative proposals or language that is not accepted by one of the parties. Both sides usually want to lock in the other side's key commitments as early as possible.
- *The order of implementation*. The order for implementing the interrelated parts of a complicated peace agreement may be the single most crucial factor in determining the course of a peace process. Each side wants to require the other side to take early, irreversible steps. Although, strictly speaking, implementation takes place after the negotiation is concluded, mediators often find that some agreed actions can be taken before an overall peace accord is achieved.

These three timelines can be made to interact dynamically. A skillful mediator can—by pacing the separate agendas for exploring options, making commitments, and implementing—put together potential deals. At one extreme, each issue is discussed separately, decided on, and perhaps even implemented before the next issue is raised; this procedure makes it very hard to identify trade-offs. At the other extreme, all issues are explored but no commitments made before a single package deal is constructed; this method makes it very hard to build trust. Usually a mediator tries to navigate between these two extremes. In ordering the process of implementation, which need not follow the order of negotiation, the parties ideally are required to move forward in parallel, taking irreversible steps as early as possible.

Of course, during negotiations the mediators retain other responsibilities. For example, in the Mozambique peace process the status of the two parties—a question that had been finessed by selecting a mediator without diplomatic standing—might require definition. Once the parties began to discuss implementation, they might want to involve other governments or the United Nations, and the mediators could then coordinate an expansion of the negotiating framework.

Perhaps even more difficult than ordering the sequence of events is keeping the process moving forward. It is too easy for negotiations to take on a life of their own, becoming divorced from the reality of the conflict on the ground and losing any sense of urgency. Mediators, who often have no real leverage over the parties, then have difficulty generating and maintaining momentum.

Guebuza and Domingos had read into the record the previous August each side's proposal for the order of implementation. The government wanted first a cease-fire and then reintegration of all Mozambicans into the system being reformed by the government. RENAMO wanted first a detailed commitment to change the system, followed by a cease-fire and then elections. Because RENAMO held that only the threat of military action gave it leverage in the negotiations and because this leverage would be lost at the outset of the process of implementation, RENAMO insisted that cease-fire arrangements be discussed last.

Round Four: January 29–31, 1991

The December 1 agreement was intended to reduce conflict by limiting the activity of Zimbabwean troops in Mozambique and by stopping attacks on the transport corridors. The operation of the JVC, by building trust between the parties, was expected to give additional impetus to the entire peace process. Events during January challenged these expectations.

On January 17, 1991, the chairman of the JVC, Ambassador Incisa, signed a report covering the activity of the JVC and its military committee up to that date. This report documented individual incidents and recommended what uses of the corridors should be permitted, where the exact boundaries of the corridors should be, and what authority the JVC should have to investigate incidents anywhere in Mozambique that seemed counter to the spirit of the December 1 agreement.

The chairman's report differed in one important respect from the practice followed by the UN secretary-general in reporting on peacekeeping operations. The JVC aimed to follow the practices of UN peacekeepers by investigating all reports of incidents. The secretary-general normally indicates in the factual chapter of such reports only the receipt of allegations of individual incidents and actions to investigate. He does not seek to identify precisely the responsibility for individual incidents, and any judgments he makes go into a separate, brief section entitled "Observations." The first report by the chairman of the JVC mentioned investigations of eight incidents; it included the judgment that RENAMO was "very likely" responsible for six of the attacks, while there was insufficient evidence in the other two cases to determine responsibility.

The chairman's report, in seeking to clarify the unresolved issue of military use of the corridors, proposed a definition of "military operations of an offensive nature" that would have a severe impact on RENAMO, some impact on Zimbabwean forces, but no impact on the FAM: "Each and every occasion on which RENAMO fighters enter the corridors for any reason without written authorization from the JVC; or whenever RENAMO fires weapons inside the corridors; each and every occasion on which Zimbabwean troops move outside the corridors, with the exception, should the negotiators agree, of Combomune and Mapai in the Limpopo corridor; and, whenever Zimbabwean troops fire weapons outside the corridors. . . . Any crossing through the corridors by RENAMO without notification as well as reconnaissance missions by Zimbabwean troops outside the corridors, or by RENAMO forces inside the corridors, shall be considered hostile acts." Zimbabwe agreed to provide notice to the JVC's military committee of any planned movements involving more than 135 of its troops. The members of the JVC, all ambassadors accredited to the government of Mozambique, recommended no steps to restrict any activity by the FAM, perhaps because the government considered such restrictions to be unacceptable infringements of national sovereignty.

General Pascoal Jose, RENAMO's representative on the JVC, failed to have RENAMO's interests taken into account.

The report recognized that the Chimoio airport (used by Zimbabwean forces for resupply) was outside the corridor but called for agreement to ensure the safety of airport operations. It recommended extensions of the corridors to include logistical assets, such as power lines and water sources (an extension that Domingos had already rejected during the December negotiations in Rome). The report noted with satisfaction that no incidents had been reported during the period January 10–17.

Although the JVC had no explicit mandate to do so, the report took note of the murder of Portuguese missionary Father Manuel Joaquim Cristovao on January 21 in an ambush outside the corridors. In keeping with the "spirit" of the December 1 agreement, the JVC condemned this act. Moreover, citing language in article IV of the agreement that gave the JVC responsibility for encouraging the establishment of peace, the report urged the parties to refrain from hostile acts anywhere. The chairman announced that the JVC would entrust its military committee "with investigations of incidents outside the corridors that violate the spirit of the Rome Agreement and the process of establishing peace."

On January 22 Ambassador Incisa sent to Don Matteo Zuppi his personal evaluation of the work of the JVC. Incisa complained that the British and to a lesser extent the U.S. members of the JVC were too ready to attribute any attack along the corridors to RENAMO, despite the known existence of other armed groups in the area and the reputation of government forces for occasional attacks on civilians. Incisa wrote that the JVC was "an instrument that to the extent possible should build trust between the parties and not jump to conclusions."[1]

When the two delegations returned to Rome to resume talks on January 29, the first item on the agenda was the report by the JVC's chairman. Speaking for the government, Guebuza agreed with the report's recommendations on the definition of the corridors and on the nature of prohibited offensive military activity. As for RENAMO charges regarding presence and activities of Zimbabwean troops outside the corridors, Guebuza acknowledged the JVC's decision that these charges should be investigated. He endorsed the stated intention of the JVC to investigate incidents anywhere in the country that seemed to jeopardize the peace process.

RENAMO's response was critical. Domingos emphasized the importance of the work of the JVC as a vehicle for building trust between the two sides. He criticized all the recommendations in the report because they went beyond the powers of a technical body. The JVC should apply, not amend, the obligations specified in the December 1 agreement. Domingos asked the JVC to respect the need for impartiality in its work. Although the report noted charges that the government was in violation of the agreement because of the presence of Zimbabwean troops outside the corridors, the JVC had not investigated this charge. Domingos regretted the lack of reports on the presence of Zimbabwean troops at the Chimoio airport. Even the JVC, by recommending that this airport be treated as if it were inside the Beira corridor, acknowledged that it was outside the corridor. If the members of the JVC had reason to use the Chimoio airport to support an investigation mission, both sides could clear this use in advance. As proof of RENAMO's good faith and ability to implement local cease-fires, Domingos cited RENAMO's faithful implementation since August 22, 1989, of the agreement it had reached with Malawi to refrain from attacks on the Nacala corridor as a gesture of goodwill.

Away from the negotiating table, Domingos freely expressed his negative judgments on the JVC. None of its members, even those named by RENAMO, had spoken up to defend RENAMO's interests. He turned aside advice that RENAMO should strengthen its representation on the JVC by sending a political representative to Maputo. Domingos insisted political issues were to be discussed only through the Rome talks, and from his perspective there was no reason to enhance the authority of the JVC by sending a political representative to Maputo. When asked whether RENAMO would agree to exercise restraint in attacks on the Tete corridor between Zimbabwe and Malawi in order to facilitate ICRC activities in the area, he recalled that RENAMO had not committed itself to restraint in the Tete corridor and could not do so because the FAM used the corridor to reinforce its units.

Domingos refused to discuss political issues until RENAMO's need for secure communication between Rome and Gorongosa had been satisfied. He threatened renewed RENAMO attacks because Zimbabwean troops were not yet concentrated in the corridors. Guebuza rejected RENAMO's complaints about the implementation of the December 1 agreement and the work of the JVC and criticized Domingos's refusal to discuss political issues until there was a secure Rome-Gorongosa communication link.

After two unproductive sessions, the mediators suspended the talks. In addition to the problems on the table, the mediators were concerned that RENAMO was unprepared to negotiate the political items, such as the political party law, due for discussion next. RENAMO, while it espoused a commitment to democratic principles, had no experience in negotiating for the kind of practical arrangements and compromises needed to give these policies concrete meaning. Domingos and the delegation in Rome did not have adequate authority to negotiate these questions on their own, and thus the secure communication link might be required for any prolonged discussions. A rumor that the government of Zambia was trying to arrange a summit meeting between Chissano and Dhlakama looked like another distraction.

The mediators extracted from both sides authority to issue a press statement indicating that "the mediators invited the parties to pause for reflection to give delegations a chance to consider and evaluate the reciprocal positions before the next meeting of the talks."

So far the implementation of the December 1 agreement had not built any trust. The mediators wanted to reconvene talks as soon as the secure Rome-Gorongosa communication link was working. The U.S. observer, now Cameron Hume, encouraged the mediators to pressure RENAMO to define its goals and objectives for a political program, which would be needed to keep the negotiations moving forward. In turn the mediators asked that the United States support their efforts and urge the parties to move forward in the talks without delay. President Chissano had already signed a draft law that would permit registration of political parties.

Maneuvering: February to April 1991

For several months the issues left unresolved in January troubled the atmosphere for negotiations. On February 8 General Pascoal Jose, RENAMO's representative to the JVC, told a JVC meeting that RENAMO did not accept any of its recommendations to extend the corridors because doing so would increase Zimbabwean control over Mozambican territory. Therefore, RENAMO rejected including the Chimoio airport in the Beira corridor, as well as the judgment that the presence of Zimbabwean troops at the airport was only a technical violation of the agreement. The JVC adopted a statement taking note of RENAMO's position but concluding that "Zimbabwean forces should have continuing, secure access to the Chimoio airport."

JVC meetings on February 19, 21, and 28 gave RENAMO no satisfaction. The first recorded that the five investigations of RENAMO's charges that there were Zimbabwean forces outside the corridors had not confirmed the allegations—but of course the investigations could only take place several days after the government had been informed of the decision to investigate. Meanwhile it looked as if Zimbabwean forces were actually building new facilities at the Chimoio airport. The February 21 meeting adopted a statement claiming that the JVC had a major role as an instrument in the peace process beyond its specific responsibilities for the corridors; a second statement recommended that the government take over responsibility for the Chimoio airport from Zimbabwean forces. At the third meeting the Mozambican government delegation registered its view that "the airport of Chimoio is part of the Beira Corridor."

On March 4 Dhlakama's office issued a communique addressed to the governments of Mozambique and Zimbabwe. It announced that because Zimbabwean troops inside Mozambique continued to operate outside the corridors despite the obligations of the December 1 agreement, RENAMO had been obliged to resume attacks against the Limpopo corridor on February 23. RENAMO threatened to resume attacks against the Beira corridor as well if Zimbabwean troops were not withdrawn before April 5. In an interview on the Voice of America on March 5 Dhlakama repeated the substance of this communique. He said that he was currently outside Mozambique conducting a diplomatic offensive to explain the situation to those governments that still took the Marxist government of Mozambique at its word. On March 8 the JVC, meeting in Maputo, adopted a statement rejecting RENAMO's threats to attack the corridors.

Dhlakama came to Rome on March 8 and the next day met with U.S. observer Hume. Dhlakama expressed satisfaction that both sides now wanted peace and that they agreed that multiparty elections would be the basis of the new political system. There was still the problem of Zimbabwean troops in Mozambique operating outside the corridors. He said RENAMO's delegation was prepared to discuss political issues, which might include what form of transition government would be needed to conduct the multiparty elections.

Two days later Dhlakama met for two hours with Cohen's principal deputy assistant secretary, Ambassador Jeffrey Davidow. Dhlakama, after explaining why he was dissatisfied with the implementation of the December 1 agreement, said he could not consent to a cease-fire until there was a political agreement. Nor would RENAMO accept the new FRELIMO constitution or political party laws promulgated without any input from RENAMO. After Dhlakama admitted that RENAMO had more experience in military than in political affairs, Davidow urged him to expedite the development of RENAMO as a political organization with its positions prepared for political negotiations.

Before Dhlakama left Rome on March 18, he expanded his circle of diplomatic contacts. For the first time he met with Prime Minister Andreotti, with Soviet ambassador Anatoly Adamishin, and with the Holy

See's deputy foreign minister, Monsignor Claudio Celli. Dhlakama told the mediators that he would send a political representative to Maputo to strengthen RENAMO's representation on the JVC. Once the secure communication link from Gorongosa to Rome was working, political discussions could resume in Rome. He authorized the mediators to release a communique on March 20 announcing the proximate resumption of negotiations in Rome "in order to confront all the political problems on the agenda."

Dhlakama asked Sant'Egidio to help set up a meeting between representatives of RENAMO and Zimbabwe. After initial contacts through church channels, Sant'Egidio arranged for Domingos to meet a Zimbabwean delegation on April 28 in Rome.

Before the JVC next met on April 10, a RENAMO spokesman announced that, despite the ultimatum of March 4, as a "goodwill gesture" RENAMO forces would not attack the Beira corridor. During the meeting General Jose firmly denied that RENAMO forces had committed a recent attack at Machipanda near the Zimbabwean border. He announced that in the next round of talks in Rome RENAMO would not make an issue of Zimbabwean forces in Mozambique and that this problem could be addressed later in the context of a cease-fire. It seems that RENAMO, in its own way, had used the ultimatum and its suspension to signal a readiness to open direct communication with Zimbabwe on the role of its forces inside Mozambique.

In the first four months the arrangements for the JVC had shown their limitations. A cease-fire restricted to two corridors was inherently unstable, permitting untrammeled fighting elsewhere in the country. It was vulnerable to conflicts over technical definitions: What was offensive action? Were there any restrictions on the FAM's use of the corridors? Was it reasonable to prohibit movement through the corridors by RENAMO forces unless notification were first given to the FAM? With the resources at hand, the JVC could not fully monitor these arrangements. The December 1 agreement had opened a dialogue between RENAMO and Zimbabwe, but it had built no trust between RENAMO and the government.

Although the Rome negotiations were blocked during this period, both the government and RENAMO worked to prepare their positions for upcoming negotiations on political issues. President Chissano had launched the government's preparations for political talks with RENAMO starting with the January 1, 1988, amnesty. In July 1989 FRELIMO's fifth party congress abandoned Marxism-Leninism as its official doctrine and endorsed a proposal for negotiations with RENAMO. Subsequently the government adopted a constitution that provided for multi-party elections, and in

December 1990 the Assembly of the Republic approved the new law on political parties that provided for their registration, autonomy, funding, and activities. However, Chissano delayed promulgating this law in view of the anticipated negotiations with RENAMO on political issues.

RENAMO looked to outside legal experts, including U.S. constitutional lawyer Bruce Fein and Professor Andre Thomashausen of South Africa's Witwatersrand University, to help develop and publicize RENAMO's political program. After consultations in Kenya with Dhlakama and other RENAMO advisers, preparation of three political documents began. The first was a draft constitution that would establish a new government "in commemoration of the brave and valiant who fought both foreign and domestic oppressors and despoilers of our venerable nation . . . [and] to establish a rule of law, secure individual liberty, promote economic prosperity, and to establish democratic political institutions to live for the ages." When this document was published in July 1991, Dhlakama explained in a preface that it contained RENAMO's political agenda: "the creation of political and economic institutions and iron-clad protection of fundamental human rights."

The second document was a seventy-two-page, article-by-article critique of the new Mozambican constitution. This document was published, also in July, under the title "The Dhlakama Papers." In the preface Dhlakama explained, "My earnest desire is that Mozambique carry the torch of democracy to Africa, and simultaneously discredit the canard that Black Africans are ill-suited for the responsible exercise of self-government."

The third document produced for RENAMO during the spring of 1991 was a plan for the transition period between a cease-fire and elections. The model for this document was the elaborate UN operation for Cambodia, which in essence transferred administrative authority from the government of the nation-state to an international mechanism. The choice of this option reflected the depth of RENAMO's skepticism that the FRELIMO government, operating under a FRELIMO constitution, could be trusted to conduct fair, multiparty elections. The government was vehemently opposed to intrusive international administration of the country because this would constitute a massive infringement of national sovereignty. Closing the gap on this issue would require constant effort.

Round Five: May 6 to June 7, 1991

To prepare for resumed negotiations the mediators had traveled to the region to meet with the leaders of both sides. In mid-February, Raffaelli,

Goncalves, and Zuppi met with Dhlakama in Malawi and then with Chissano in Maputo. The mediators presented both sides with an outline agenda for talks on political and military issues. They were optimistic that both sides would approach the work ahead with a practical spirit.

Dhlakama insisted that the government's legislation on political issues, such as its recently adopted political party law, had no legitimacy because the legislature was not elected through a democratic process. However, he did not insist that the negotiators in Rome had to reconcile each point on political issues in detail. The mediators wondered whether RENAMO's draft constitution might be a useful document if used flexibly as a point of reference in preparing negotiating positions.

Raffaelli saw that the way forward was to get the parties to agree on the main principles, to let the government retain responsibility for legislation and administration, and to involve the international community in monitoring and guaranteeing implementation.

Chissano acknowledged that the agenda for the talks could put political issues before negotiations for a cease-fire. He would accept international monitoring of a cease-fire and elections, perhaps by the United Nations. He was willing to accept coordination of the process of implementation by a mixed commission composed of representatives of the government, RENAMO, and perhaps the United Nations. Chissano acknowledged that the government's recently adopted law on political parties would probably have to be amended to get RENAMO on board.

By April, Dhlakama signaled that he wanted to strengthen RENAMO's negotiating position by breaking out of his relative diplomatic isolation. When Chissano visited Kenya in April to meet with President Moi, Permanent Secretary Kiplagat tried unsuccessfully to arrange a meeting between Chissano and Dhlakama, who was then residing in Kenya. At the end of April, Dhlakama visited Lisbon, where his family was staying.

In the week before negotiations resumed, Dhlakama went to Geneva for meetings with the ICRC. He approved in principle proposals for ICRC convoys to escort food deliveries through the Tete corridor from Zimbabwe to refugee camps in Malawi. A second proposal was for the ICRC to help with repatriation of refugees into the fifty-kilometer (thirty-mile) band of territory near the Malawi border, with the possibility that the JVC could help with verification. (In fact the JVC did not have the capacity to conduct such monitoring.) The government, preferring that maximum effort be given to pushing for a full cease-fire, rejected this proposal. The need for humanitarian assistance was not yet painful enough to the two parties to create a sense of urgency.

Because RENAMO's secure communication link was not yet working, the opening of the round was delayed until May 6. Meanwhile, the mediators met separately with the two delegations in the hope that they could then draft a mediators' proposal on the political party law and the election system. After a few days in Rome, the government delegation was chafing at RENAMO's refusal to meet until the radio link was working, and it considered that RENAMO had no substantive reason to object to the government's new political party law. RENAMO, in its initial talks with the mediators, did not focus on details of the laws but insisted on overall political guarantees, such as the elimination of the security service (SNASP). The U.S. observer advised the mediators first to draw out the parties so that their positions were on the table; then the mediators could chose how best to move the negotiations forward.

On the afternoon of May 6 the round formally began with a plenary session at Sant'Egidio. Guebuza affirmed that the government wanted a negotiated solution, but he insisted that the legitimacy of the government not be questioned by the peace process. Domingos promised a full commitment to the negotiating process and then read out specific RENAMO requirements:

- The terms for multiparty elections and for a cease-fire must be negotiated.
- Once agreement on these points was reached, RENAMO would participate in an immediate cease-fire.
- There should be a one-year period between the start of the cease-fire and the elections.
- Both sides should pledge themselves to respect freedom of the press and of association.
- A small national army would be formed to replace the forces of FRELIMO and RENAMO, the regular police force would be depoliticized, and SNASP would be demobilized.
- The purpose of the present round of negotiations would be "to establish a basis for resolving these problems and to draw up the calendar for the chronological order of discussion."

The mediators thought that they could finesse some of the contradictions between the two positions. They planned to draft a detailed agenda to order the discussion and resolution of one group of issues after another, building confidence and momentum before the talks arrived at military issues. Although RENAMO demanded that the political party and electoral laws be discussed and general principles be agreed on, it did not demand a right to participate in the drafting of the actual legislation or to approve a specific text in detail.

By May 13 the talks, after several days of nearly continuous meetings, reached a deadlock over the apparently simple issue of specifying in an agenda the items to be discussed. Because of the government's insistence on respect for national sovereignty, Guebuza rejected a subitem on a mixed commission to supervise a cease-fire and elections. Domingos, who had initially preferred a simple, open-ended agenda, now wanted the agenda to be a signed, detailed document; everything part of the peace process had to be specified, and what was not specified could not be included later.

Both sides agreed that the agenda should include items on political party law, the election system, forming a national army, a cease-fire, guarantees for the process of implementation, a donors conference, and signing the final protocol declaring a general peace. RENAMO then insisted on including as subitems the elimination of SNASP, repatriation of refugees, liberation of political prisoners, and abolition of private armies. The government rejected these subitems. When the mediators tried more neutral formulations, RENAMO insisted on language specifying the purpose of the discussion.

Flexibility was disappearing. The level of mutual distrust was rising, depriving the mediators of the control normally ceded to a mediator to manage the agenda. The emerging agenda created a rigid paradigm for future negotiations. Neither side was comfortable with a more fluid format. The mediators were worried about how this impasse would affect the need to renew the December 1, 1990, agreement by June 1, when it was scheduled to expire.

Assistant Secretary Cohen came to Rome on May 16 to meet with the mediators and parties. He suggested to Domingos that RENAMO accept neutral formulations of proposed agenda items in language that was non-threatening and non-prejudicial. Domingos explained that for RENAMO cadres to feel safe in returning to civilian life they needed the elimination of SNASP, not just its reform. Guebuza told Cohen that the government could accept discussion of the items proposed by RENAMO, but it would not allow them to be framed in a way that would prejudice the outcome. The mediators told Cohen that to break this impasse they would prepare an amended agenda that described the items for discussion in neutral language and that postponed discussion of the troublesome subitems on political prisoners, private armies, and SNASP until the agenda item on military issues.

The mediators decided that to break the deadlock they would have to speak directly with Dhlakama, as they had done the previous November to get the partial cease-fire agreement of December 1. Raffaelli, Goncalves, and Zuppi made an appointment to meet Dhlakama in Malawi. To give additional backing to the mediators, Assistant Secretary Cohen sent Dhlakama a letter supporting their approach asking that RENAMO look favorably on an extension of the December 1 agreement. When the mediators met with Dhlakama on the night of May 22, he told them he had "no problem" with their new draft for an agenda and that Domingos, who was present for the meeting, would return to Rome on May 25. However, Dhlakama repeated his position that the laws on political issues adopted by the national assembly in Maputo were null and void and that such legislation would have to be revised through the negotiations in Rome. This position threatened to paralyze the negotiations by denying the government's legitimacy, and the mediators would have to find some way to contain this threat in order for the negotiations to bear fruit.

Raffaelli, Goncalves, and Zuppi then went to Maputo to review with President Chissano the status of the negotiations and to seek agreement on the agenda and on renewing the December 1 agreement. During their meeting Raffaelli explained his preference to push RENAMO for concrete signs that it accepted the current constitution as the legitimate framework for whatever arrangements might be agreed to during the negotiations. He wanted to secure explicit agreement on each agenda item as the parties worked through the agenda. Goncalves had already urged a different approach that would include the sequential discussion of individual items but permit RENAMO to postpone any commitment on the legitimacy of the new constitution. President Chissano agreed with Goncalves's approach, explaining that he did not want to force RENAMO to reject now a commitment that it might well accept later.

The mediators then returned to Rome and resumed their contacts with the two delegations. On May 28 they announced agreement on a detailed agenda. The items that RENAMO had insisted on were included, but in neutral language as insisted on by the government. The sequence of the items was that proposed by the mediators in their compromise approach, including the thorny issue of the security service in the item on military issues that would be discussed after political questions but before the cease-fire. The order of the six main items on the agenda was (1) the law on political parties, (2) the electoral system, (3) military issues (including formation of a unified national army), (4) a cease-fire, (5) guarantees, and (6) a donors' conference.

The parties agreed to extend the December 1 agreement indefinitely. On June 6 Zuppi told the press that the negotiations would be suspended for several weeks so that the parties could have an "interval for reflection and evaluation on their positions."

Round Six: August 1–7, 1991

The detailed agenda deprived the mediators of flexibility in managing the talks, and it did not lead to early discussions on political questions. Both sides dug in on the issue of the government's legitimacy. The FRELIMO negotiators wanted explicit acknowledgment that the government's administration of the country would be accepted by RENAMO during the period from the cease-fire until after the elections. RENAMO, which might agree not to disturb the government's administration after a cease-fire, refused to consider the FRELIMO role legitimate. From June to September the parties, the mediators, and other governments looked for ways to get past this argument and to start talks on the political party and election laws.

On June 6 Dhlakama instructed Domingos, who was still in Rome, "to put an end to the government's games." To expose the falsity of the government's pretense of encouraging democracy, Domingos should ask to go to Maputo with his delegation for one week of public meetings, radio broadcasts, and newspaper interviews. The mediators used their good offices to forward this request to Maputo. Guebuza denied the request, explaining that until there was a cease-fire the RENAMO presence in Maputo would be limited to its representative to the JVC.[2]

RENAMO consulted more with such outside experts as Bruce Fein and Andre Thomashausen to prepare texts that could be adapted for use in negotiations. Domingos obtained a copy of the Angola Accords so that he could study the arrangements on military questions.

The government, whose political program was contained in the new constitution and draft political party law, worked on other items in the agenda, and it produced a draft cease-fire agreement based on the model of the Angola Accords, modified for conditions in Mozambique. The government consulted with several donor governments to identify funding for the creation of a unified national defense force with 24,000 soldiers, plus several thousand members of the small naval and air forces. Before creating the new force, the government needed enough money to liquidate the back pay claims of the soldiers being demobilized and to give them a bonus to ease their transition to civilian life. More than half the FAM troops plus thousands of RENAMO fighters would have to be paid off.

The interruption of the Rome talks in June stimulated a round of consultations among those governments that had already demonstrated an interest in the negotiations. Portugal and the United States, fresh from the conclusion of the Angola negotiations, questioned whether reinforcing the international framework for the talks (so far limited to the four mediators, with logistical support from the Italian government) could speed up progress. They were concerned that the low-profile mediation had started out with little leverage over the parties and that the detailed agenda weakened the mediators' ability to influence the negotiating process.

In mid-June the State Department sent Deputy Assistant Secretary Davidow and a team of military and political experts to meet President Chissano and other Mozambican officials in Maputo. They hoped to meet Dhlakama and RENAMO officials either in Europe or at a convenient site in Africa. In these discussions the U.S. side wanted to draw out the parties on their views and to provide information on how the Angola agreements had been reached and on how they would be implemented. Davidow wanted to come to Rome to exchange views with the mediators on possible ways forward, which might include giving more prominence to the U.S. role and inviting an official Portuguese presence.

Dhlakama, who wanted to use international contacts to enhance his prestige, explained that he would be glad to receive the U.S. delegation in Gorongosa but that he was too busy to be away from RENAMO's general headquarters for the time being. The U.S. side declined the suggestion that it travel to Gorongosa and insisted on a neutral site.

When Assistant Secretary Cohen traveled to Lisbon for a conference on Portuguese-speaking Africa on June 21–23, he planned to consult separately with Portugal's Secretary of State for Cooperation Jose Durao Barroso and with Raffaelli on the status of the talks in Rome. The Portuguese, while not opposing the Italian mediation, wanted Portugal and the United States to have a significant formal role, one commensurate with the success they had just registered working together on Angola. Mozambique was obviously a subject of considerable interest in Portuguese politics.

Raffaelli met separately with Cohen and with Durao Barroso. Raffaelli thought that it was best to work through the items on the agenda regarding the political party law and elections before enlarging the format for the talks to include participation by U.S. and Portuguese officials. The United States and Portugal might become official observers when discussion turned to military questions, and Portugal in particular might look to a role in forming the new national army. Raffaelli cautioned that of course the parties would have to consent to the addition of official observers to the talks. For the time being the greatest challenge was to convince RENAMO to accept that the government, monitored by some international mechanism, would administer the election fairly. Raffaelli acknowledged to Cohen the need for increased international participation and expressed appreciation for U.S. support for the mediators, but he said he was less certain what role Portugal would play.

Davidow and the team left Washington on July 7. Their first stop was Rome, where they met with both Italian government officials and the mediators. Davidow then went to South Africa, where key leaders expressed their support for the Rome negotiating process. They explained that the South African ambassador in Rome, Glenn Babb, had maintained contact with the government delegation, but that since earlier in the year, RENAMO's delegation had refused contact with South African officials.

Davidow was in Maputo on July 10 and 11. He met with President Chissano, as well as separately with FAM chief of staff Lieutenant General Antonio Hama Thai, Brigadier General Tobias Dai, and Minister Guebuza. The government was frustrated at RENAMO's stop-and-go negotiating tactics. They complained that RENAMO had caused the break in the negotiations at the beginning of June by refusing to accept the government's role in conducting the elections. The government could not permit the United Nations to be responsible for registering parties or conducting the elections. Davidow recalled that in the Angolan case a comparable deadlock was broken when UNITA accepted the legitimacy of the government and the government accepted UNITA as a political party. The correct formula still had to be found to articulate the same basic deal for Mozambique: legitimacy for the government and a privileged role in the peace process for its main opposition.

Dhlakama was unavailable to meet with Davidow either in Rome or in any African location outside Gorongosa.

By the third week of July both negotiating delegations returned to Rome. The government came eager to enter into detailed discussion of the political items on the agenda; RENAMO came with suspicions that the government's recent bombing of the airstrip at Gorongosa had been an attempt to kill Dhlakama. On July 22 Dhlakama sent Domingos a message reminding his negotiator that, because no outside government supported RENAMO, his side should not be subjected to pressure. In any case, the two negotiating teams and the mediators had an informal dinner together at Sant'Egidio on July 25, and the atmosphere between the two sides seemed good.

The mediators conducted bilateral discussions with both teams to find a way to bridge the gap between the government's insistence that arrangements for implementation not denigrate its legitimacy in any way and RENAMO's refusal to acknowledge the government's legitimacy. The mediators produced and gave to both sides a draft protocol entitled "On Fundamental Principles." The main elements in the draft were as follows:

- The government would commit itself not to act contrary to the terms of protocols agreed to and not to adopt laws contrary to such protocols.
- From the date of a cease-fire, RENAMO would respect existing laws and institutions, including the state and the government.
- Both parties agreed to work to complete negotiation of the items on the May 28 agenda as quickly as possible.
- A joint military-political commission, including a representative of the United Nations, would be established by the general peace agreement.

On August 1 the seventh round of peace talks was opened in a formal session at the Foreign Ministry's Villa Madama, a Medici villa on Monte Mario overlooking Rome. The mediators hoped to use this formal session to create a sense of urgency in the talks and to signal the backing provided by the Italian government.

In the days that followed, the government delegation criticized the draft because it came too close to infringing its sovereignty. Where was the assembly that made the laws—in Rome or in Maputo? But Guebuza signaled that the text might be acceptable as long as it was understood that any agreement reached in Rome would have to be submitted to the assembly for ratification and that the drafting of actual legislation would be left for the government and assembly.

Domingos, who received new instructions from Dhlakama on August 3, rejected the proposed text and broke off the talks. Dhlakama's long fax claimed that it would be suicide for RENAMO to negotiate on the basis of the mediators' draft. In a rambling analysis the fundamental objection appeared repeatedly: FRELIMO could not be trusted to do in Maputo what it promised in Rome.[3]

In a letter to a Vatican diplomat on August 12, Zuppi said the mediators had been convinced RENAMO would have agreed to the draft. What went wrong? There was too much distrust between the two sides, and RENAMO had a "deep fear of falling into the trap of integration." In addition it was too hard for the mediators to communicate with Dhlakama, who would make all substantial decisions, and to explain this text. Finally

RENAMO, perhaps because of an upcoming FRELIMO congress, simply wanted to stall for time.[4]

The mediators asked the departing delegations to reflect on the proposal before them and to prepare positions for discussion of a political party law and the election system.[5]

The mediators knew that they were operating within a weak framework. The parties could do as they liked. A more structured international framework would constrain at least the procedural choices available to the parties. Of course the parties should make their own choices on questions of substance, but there was little point in having a mediator with no control over process or timing. Outside parties with interests but no place at the table—including at least the United States, Portugal, Zimbabwe, Kenya, South Africa, and Britain—might try to alter or even to replace the Rome format for the talks if the two sides continued to stall. Aware of the important role the United States could play in sustaining the Rome talks, the mediators confirmed U.S. support. Next, they sought a meeting with Dhlakama.

Round Seven: October 1–18, 1991

On August 22 RENAMO sent a message to Sant'Egidio that reported a concentration of FRELIMO forces and a Zimbabwean battalion in the area of Canganitole with the presumed mission of launching an attack on RENAMO bases in the Gorongosa area. RENAMO asked the mediators to forward the message to Ambassador Incisa so that he could inform the members of the JVC in his role as chairman. Should the attack be launched, RENAMO forces would retaliate against the Beira corridor.

A week later RENAMO's presidential cabinet again communicated with the mediators. The message urged the mediators to meet with Dhlakama, preferably in Gorongosa. He had traveled several times to Rome, and his visits had helped with the peace process. Of course the work of the mediators was difficult and needed more understanding and support from the international community. The mediators should convince the government that, within the framework of the peace process, Dhlakama should be able to meet with the mediators and other interested parties in "Gorongosa, Paris, Washington, or Rome." It would not be a violation of Mozambique's sovereignty for visitors to come to Gorongosa, because everyone knew there was only one Mozambican sovereignty and the visits would in any case be in the context of the peace process. That said, for the immediate future Dhlakama's responsibilities would not permit him to travel away from Gorongosa.

To explain their draft, the mediators wanted to meet with Dhlakama before talks resumed in Rome, but they did not want to go to Gorongosa to do so. They thought Dhlakama's main reason for this demand was to boost his own status, and they knew that the government would object strenuously.

In early September, Kenya's Bethuel Kiplagat, with whom Zuppi had met on August 24 in Geneva to review the status of the talks, offered to draw Dhlakama out of Gorongosa to meet with Davidow. Washington answered that Davidow still wanted the meeting to support the negotiations in Rome and had no intention of doing anything to replace the Italian mediation. Dhlakama would have to be out of the bush before anyone left Washington.

The mediators thought Dhlakama was beginning to feel weakened by his self-imposed isolation. Upon hearing that he might be willing to meet outside Mozambique, they set off in the hope that they could persuade him to accept the draft they had proposed in August to get around the constant argument over legitimacy. Perhaps the unproductive consequences of his isolation had made him more susceptible to a settlement on this point. They intended to emphasize to Dhlakama the benefit of having the government accept in this draft the involvement of the United Nations in the joint military-political commission that would oversee the entire process of implementation. Even if he were to agree, they were apprehensive that the RENAMO leader would discover other impediments to the talks. On September 20, 1991, Raffaelli, Goncalves, and Zuppi met with Dhlakama in Malawi.[6]

Dhlakama now looked at the draft in a positive light, but he wanted to add a clause obliging the government not to hinder RENAMO's international contacts. The mediators would see what they could do.

While in the region the mediators met on September 21 with President Chissano in Maputo and on September 23 with President Moi in Nairobi. Now a deal seemed possible, and negotiations were set to resume at the beginning of October.

Davidow and Townsend B. Friedman, Jr., the U.S. ambassador in Maputo, visited Rome on October 3 and 4 to meet with the mediators and the two delegations, who had already returned to Rome for the seventh round of talks. Davidow restated his desire to meet with Dhlakama. The United States, Davidow explained, wanted to re-animate the peace process and to give the parties some sense of urgency. Neither side had any prospect of military success, and another year of drought was making the humanitarian situation worse. With the mediators he floated the idea of a general meeting of interested governments that would operate as an informal review conference one year after the conclusion of the December 1 agreement. Such a meeting might be useful even without Mozambican participation, and it could energize the peace process, perhaps by forming a contact group. The mediators were favorable to the idea of forming a contact group of interested governments in a position to support the peace process.

On October 18 the two sides signed Protocol I, the political preamble on which the negotiations had been stalled since June. Dhlakama accepted the mediators' formula, amended to include a promise by the government not to hinder RENAMO's international contacts. The government agreed "not to impede the contacts of RENAMO in the framework of the peace negotiations" and to consider, on a case-by-case basis, contacts between the mediators or members of the JVC inside the country. No one soon took up the option of visiting Dhlakama in his lair, nor did he again isolate himself in Gorongosa in order to force international contacts to come to RENAMO headquarters.

The two sides planned to resume meetings in plenary session on Tuesday, October 21, to begin discussion of the first agenda item. Underlying the discussion of the political party law was the constant dispute over legitimacy: Would RENAMO consent to register itself with FRELIMO government officials, or would it insist that there be some other way to grant recognition of its status as a political party? At least in Protocol I RENAMO had accepted a basis for leaving behind its earlier request that the United Nations run an interim government, more or less along the model for Cambodia.

On October 21 the Department of State press office posted a statement welcoming Protocol I as "an important step forward." The statement explained that "the U.S. has no formal role in the peace talks but is working closely with the Italian mediators and the negotiating parties to help reach a settlement."

On the surface the negotiations made little progress during the first ten months of 1991. Not only was there no motion toward a cease-fire, but there had not even been any discussion of military issues. The December 1 agreement remained in place, but the verification mechanism, having failed to overcome the lack of trust between the parties, was moribund. No agreement was reached to alleviate the humanitarian crisis gripping the country. The agreements on the agenda and Protocol I, however important, were procedural in nature and offered no indication of when an overall settlement might be achieved.

The agenda defined the issues and the order in which they would be discussed. The parties insisted that discussion of each agenda item be concluded and an agreement signed before the next item was discussed. Perhaps the parties wanted this rigid procedure to compensate for their mutual distrust. RENAMO managed to postpone discussion of a cease-fire until after it would have commitments from the government on the new political system, on elections, on the formation of a new national army, on the reform of the police, and on the security service.

This rigid, detailed agenda surely deprived the mediators of one of the main tools for managing a peace process: pacing the three timelines for discussion, commitment, and implementation. At least the mediators had improved the chances of getting agreements on the political party law and the election law, thereby giving the talks some badly needed momentum, by putting the knotty issues of the police, the security service, and political prisoners under the item on military questions.

The breakthrough that opened the way for substantive discussions was recorded in Protocol I. Overall, both sides saw the text as defining parameters for mutual recognition or acceptance. Each side would retain its legitimacy: the government as government and RENAMO as negotiating partner and opposition party.

More operationally, Protocol I established a format for sorting out constant disputes regarding the commitments made at the negotiating table, actions elsewhere by the parties, and the relationship of the international community to the peace process. When the general peace accord was signed at the end of the negotiating process, the government would be obliged not to act contrary to the agreements reached in Rome, and RENAMO would be required to act "within the framework of the existing institutions of the State." The government accepted that a UN representative would be a member of the joint commission to be set up to supervise and control implementation of the general peace accord. Starting immediately, the government would not impede RENAMO's external contacts and contacts between RENAMO and the mediators or members of the JVC within Mozambique.

Of course these criteria were easier to state than to apply.

four

Helping Negotiations Along

Mediators are expected to facilitate dialogue between the parties. They should help the parties communicate by providing reliable means of communication, by finding clear and precise terms through which the parties can express their ideas, or by reformulating the parties' ideas into non-threatening or neutral language. Facilitation involves more than simply carrying messages back and forth.

To improve the quality of dialogue, mediators can offer other forms of support. In this case Sant'Egidio and the Italian government provided a place to meet and material support for delegations. They advised delegations on technical subjects, helping them identify, expand, and select options. Most important, by explaining the other side's point of view, they helped each side to listen, which at times was the key to unlocking an agreement.

A spokesman for the Community of Sant'Egidio, Andrea Bartoli, said that the essence of Sant'Egidio's work was to find ways to express RENAMO's ideas in terms consistent with the overall goal of reconciliation.[1] Often the language of RENAMO's initial positions was either threatening or uncompromising. The government, accustomed to legal and diplomatic language, had less need of such assistance.

The mediators managed the dialogue between the parties at several levels. They met with Presidents Chissano and Dhlakama, either to get an overview of each side's position before a negotiating round or to get final agreement on a text worked on with the delegations in Rome. Negotiating rounds began and ended with formal plenary sessions in which each side could put its position on the table; the give-and-take of negotiating was conducted by the mediators through repeated bilateral contacts with each side on the basis of a mediators' negotiating text. RENAMO refused to participate in joint working sessions until the final days of the negotiations. By keeping lines of communication open with the leaders in Mozambique as well as with the delegations in Rome, the mediators might overcome problems of communication between the leaders and their negotiators. The mediators husbanded very carefully their limited ability to influence the parties by conferring or withholding symbols of legitimacy from proposed solutions.

The mediators' role was crucial during the negotiations on the political party and election laws. They would have to lead the parties toward the middle ground, using the process of dialogue to prepare the parties for peace. They would need creativity to reduce complex issues to simple ones, postponing the harder parts for resolution later. Of course mediators cannot force reconciliation. Each party must recognize the other's right to exist, must put aside past wrongs, and must compromise.

In addition to the four mediators, other sources had been helping the negotiations along. The Kenyan government had issued passports for RENAMO representatives, and Tiny Rowland had helped with transportation for Dhlakama. The Italian government had provided travel money and political cover for the mediators, including the supporting work done by the Italian ambassador in Maputo. The United States gave technical advice, encouragement, and public support. Humanitarian assistance agencies—including the ICRC, UN agencies, and voluntary organizations—through their normal work constantly reminded the parties that only peace could stop the tragedy facing the Mozambican people.

Round Eight on Political Party Law:
October 21 to November 13, 1991

Starting in October 1991, U.S. support for the mediation became more active.

After signing Protocol I, RENAMO wanted to take advantage of the clause committing the government not to impede RENAMO's international contacts. Over the next few weeks Dhlakama traveled to Geneva, Lisbon, and Rome. Because of the progress in the peace process, RENAMO wanted the United States to review its position prohibiting Dhlakama from visiting the United States. In fact, because of its commitment to a negotiated peace, RENAMO now felt that it merited political, financial, and diplomatic help from the international community.

The United States decided to increase its own involvement in the talks. On October 31 Deputy Assistant Secretary Davidow brought with him to Rome a delegation that included Ambassador Friedman from Maputo and four experts from Washington who had been involved in the Angola negotiations. Davidow wanted to meet with the mediators and the government delegation, as well as to touch base at the Italian Foreign Ministry. After Rome, Davidow planned to meet in Geneva with Dhlakama and the RENAMO negotiating team on November 1 and 2, meetings that would constitute the technical consultations that had been postponed since June because Dhlakama had insisted on a meeting in Gorongosa.

In Rome, Davidow concentrated on the issue of finding the best format for lining up the support of additional governments for the peace process. Raffaelli said he thought the United States could increase the profile of its support for the negotiations, perhaps even assuming some formal role, without replacing the mediators. Raffaelli, aware that other outside governments had interests at stake, suggested that an informal meeting of representatives of these governments might solidify a framework of international support.

Davidow responded that such a meeting could both strengthen the mediators' hand in the negotiations and bring on board outside governments who could later help to implement an agreement. Davidow advised the mediators to resist RENAMO's desire for an extensive UN peacekeeping mission or direct UN role in administration. It made more sense for the parties to be responsible for implementing the process they agreed on, as in Angola, with the United Nations providing outside support. Davidow told Raffaelli that he had instructed Cameron Hume, the deputy chief of mission at the U.S. embassy to the Holy See, to give all possible support to the mediators.

On November 1 Davidow and accompanying delegation met in Geneva with Dhlakama, who was joined by Raul Domingos, Vicente Ululu, and two other RENAMO officials. Dhlakama opened the talks by stating that Protocol I of October 18 constituted recognition by RENAMO of the government. RENAMO was committed to peace and to the democratization of Mozambique, but it needed assurances for its security and for the implementation of any agreement—assurances that could be provided only by more international involvement in the peace process and by more international exposure for RENAMO.

Dhlakama preferred that the Italian government explicitly take the leading role among the mediators. The United States should be more involved, along the lines of its support for Portuguese mediation in the

Angola negotiations. Portugal could be added to the talks as an observer. In commenting on the agenda items on political parties and on election laws, Dhlakama said these two items could be settled in a few weeks. It would help if expert legal advice were provided to both sides.

Davidow said the United States would consider increasing its involvement in the negotiations, but it would do so in a way that supported the Italian mediation. The international community, by working together, could provide the assurances for implementation requested by Dhlakama. To avoid the lapses in communication that had at times in the past impeded consultations between the United States and RENAMO, Davidow and Dhlakama agreed that their official contact would be through Hume and Domingos.

The next day the U.S. experts accompanying Davidow gave Dhlakama's companions a political and military briefing on the Angola agreement and arrangements for its implementation. The experts urged RENAMO to keep the talks from being bogged down in premature discussion of detail and to move quickly to a cease-fire, building momentum behind the peace process. Domingos asked questions about the arrangements for international monitoring of implementation, emphasizing that RENAMO was not satisfied with the way the December 1 agreement had been implemented. The JVC, he explained, had done nothing about Zimbabwean violations of that agreement, and RENAMO insisted that adequate arrangements were needed to monitor a general cease-fire.

In a joint press statement issued November 2, 1991, both sides expressed full support for the Italian mediation and the desire for rapid agreement on political issues and on a cease-fire. The statement indicated that the two sides had discussed how the international community could support the peace process, and Davidow offered assurances that "the United States would examine ways that it could help advance the Mozambique peace process."[2]

Ambassador Friedman stopped in Rome to brief the Italians on the meeting on his way back to Maputo. Later, throughout the next year, Friedman repeatedly used his contacts to encourage President Chissano's government to make progress in the peace talks.

Dhlakama departed for Lisbon to meet with Portuguese officials, including President Mario Soares, Prime Minister Cavaco Silva, Foreign Minister Joao de Deus Pinheiro, and Secretary of State for Cooperation Jose Durao Barroso. In public statements Dhlakama called for the Portuguese government to participate in the Rome peace process, and Durao Barroso praised the Italian mediation. Portugal, Durao Barroso explained, would consider participation in the peace process if the parties invited it to do so and if the mediators concurred.

After Domingos and Ululu returned to Rome, they handed the mediators a RENAMO proposal on the political party law and asked that it be placed on the table as the basis for discussion, displacing the draft prepared by the mediators that the parties had been discussing the previous week. RENAMO's draft, dated November 6, brought negotiations to a complete halt within forty-eight hours. This document had three parts:

- *Article One* stated that Mozambique should be transformed into a "state of democratic rights," with fundamental liberties guaranteed, including freedom of expression and a multiparty, representative political system. The political party law would be in effect only for a transition period, because the new elections would open a period of national democratic reconstruction. During the transition period, the political party law would take precedence over the constitution.
- *Article Two* defined the nature of political parties (free, autonomous citizens' organizations for the expression of democratic will), their goals (formation and expression of citizens' opinions within the political system), their rights (to function as independent organizations with full juridical status), and their obligations (to eschew violence and to support democracy and national unity).
- *Article Three* required the government to draft a law reflecting the provisions of the protocol and then to submit the draft to technical teams of both sides (making the legislative process in Maputo *ad referendum* to the talks in Rome). FRELIMO and RENAMO would automatically be registered as parties by virtue of a general peace accord.

The RENAMO draft cast doubt on RENAMO's acceptance of the government's legitimacy in the recently concluded Protocol I. The draft, although couched in lofty language, took the government to task for the previous lack of democracy. Even where the substance of RENAMO's draft agreed with the mediators' proposal, the form was different. RENAMO's draft seemed designed to complicate the negotiations and to make early agreement impossible.

Because Friedman had briefed the mediators and the government delegation on the positive meeting between Davidow and Dhlakama, both were taken aback by Domingos's presentation and his demand that they put aside the mediators' draft and work from RENAMO's proposal. The government delegation concluded that this action was a tactic to put off any possibility of agreement. Within one day, Guebuza informed the mediators that he intended to depart for Maputo because RENAMO seemed to have no interest in reaching an agreement.

The mediators alerted U.S. observer Hume that, less than a week after the Davidow-Dhlakama meeting in Geneva, the talks were breaking off. They doubted anything could still be done to keep the government delegation in Rome, and Domingos was adamant that RENAMO's draft be the basis for discussion.

To support the mediation, on November 8 Hume met first with Domingos, who was joined by Vicente Ululu and Agostinho Murrial, in the choir room at Sant'Egidio. Hume recalled that less than a week earlier Dhlakama had pledged to Davidow that the political party law could be settled quickly. After indicating that he had been informed of RENAMO's submission of a new proposal, Hume asked Domingos how the talks were progressing. Domingos described the RENAMO draft as a straightforward proposal for multiparty democracy and complained that Guebuza had refused to accept it as a basis for discussion.

Hume explained that when parties agree to a mediation, they are usually willing to work from a mediators' draft, especially after such a draft is already before the parties. If one of the parties then puts forward a competing draft, this action disrupts the negotiations and can be interpreted as a sign that the proposing party has lost faith in the mediation. Such a tactic is legitimate if one wants to get a position across in the strongest possible way, taking the risk of discrediting the mediation and perhaps breaking off the talks. To use the tactic after only a few days of talks seemed unnecessary, and it was in conflict with the position conveyed by Dhlakama to Davidow. Domingos insisted on RENAMO's right to put on the table whatever document it wanted to. While acknowledging this right, Hume suggested that a more effective tactic might be to insist that RENAMO's points be included in an amended mediators' draft. If RENAMO did not allow the mediators to resume the work of preparing the negotiating texts, it would give the unavoidable impression that RENAMO had decided to obstruct negotiations.

Next Hume met with Guebuza and the government's delegation. Guebuza said he had decided to return to Maputo in the morning. RENAMO's latest tactic left no reason for him to stay in Rome. Hume disagreed. RENAMO's tactic was disruptive, but the government delegation would give the impression that it was not committed to the negotiations if it left immediately. A better response would be to stay with the effort, listen to RENAMO's position, and then try various ways forward. If RENAMO blocked all forward paths, its bad faith would be evident to all. Unless Guebuza stayed in Rome for another week to make his case, the government's commitment to negotiations would appear in doubt to some observers. Guebuza listened.

The next day, Saturday, November 9, Guebuza canceled his travel plans, and the mediators planned to resume talks on Monday.

On Sunday, Dhlakama arrived in Rome. He did not take a direct part in the negotiations, but he had a series of meetings over the next few days: on November 11 with Monsignor Claudio Celli, the Holy See's deputy foreign minister; on November 12 with Prime Minister Giulio Andreotti; and on November 13 with Foreign Minister Gianni de Michelis. After the meeting with Andreotti, Dhlakama told a press conference that Italy should continue to be the mediator. RENAMO would accept participation by the United States and Portugal as observers, but adding more governments as observers would turn the negotiations into a conference. He told the press that RENAMO needed international guarantees for a cease-fire. "When we have laid down our weapons, who will guarantee that FRELIMO will not step back from its commitments?"

While Dhlakama was in Rome, the mediators shuttled between the RENAMO and government delegations. Gradually they achieved agreement on a version of their original proposal, amended to incorporate points from the RENAMO draft now restated in neutral language.

On November 13 the parties signed Protocol II "on the criteria and modalities for the formation and recognition of political parties." The three-and-a-half-page protocol has six parts:

- *Part one*, on the nature of political parties, states that they are independent, voluntary organizations of citizens, having an independent juridical status, organized on a democratic basis, and not espousing local or class interests.
- *Part two*, on general principles, repeats that the parties should be organized on a democratic basis and work to further national (rather than regional, tribal, separatist, racist, ethnic, or religious) interests.
- *Part three*, on rights of parties, guarantees their juridical status, freedom of expression and association of citizens, and access to the mass media.
- *Part four*, on the duties of parties, repeats that they should respect national unity and democratic principles; the choice of party names and symbols must not incite violence or racial, regional, ethnic, sexual, or religious division.
- *Part five*, on registration, states that the government will register the parties, and that 2,000 signatures will be required for registration.

- *Part six*, on implementation, states that RENAMO could begin its work as a political party as soon as a general peace agreement is signed and that a calendar for implementing this protocol would be included in the discussions under point five of the agenda (on guarantees).

Don Matteo Zuppi, in a letter to a friend written just one week later, expressed satisfaction that at last the process of mediation, now accepted by both sides, had directed the focus of discussion toward practical issues by limiting philosophical arguments. "Every so often, unfortunately, those philosophical arguments would break out . . . accentuated by mutual distrust that is still quite deep."[3]

Round Nine on Election Law: December 17–20, 1991

The mediators wanted to start negotiation of the protocol on election law as soon as possible. Because they expected the next round of talks to begin during the first week of December, the mediators gave the parties an initial draft before they left Rome to use in their preparation for the upcoming round. Raffaelli and Zuppi planned to travel to meet with Dhlakama in Blantyre and with President Chissano in Maputo before the end of November. As they had done previously, they wanted to use consultations with the leaders to narrow points of difference. For humanitarian reasons they wanted to explore with both sides the possibility of a Christmas cease-fire. Finally, they needed to talk to Chissano and Dhlakama about which other governments might be invited to participate and what role they might be asked to play when the talks reached the next agenda item on military issues.

On December 2 the mediators received a letter from Chissano requesting that France, Portugal, the United Kingdom, and the United States be asked to join the talks as official observers. Dhlakama had already accepted Portugal and the United States but not France and the United Kingdom. The mediators, aware that each additional presence at the talks would complicate their task of managing the negotiations, worried that RENAMO might add more names. In any case, because additional governments would be invited to the talks only when discussion of military issues began, no decision was yet required.

Raffaelli and Zuppi thought that their meeting with Dhlakama went well. RENAMO's leader wanted the main lines of the election law specified in the Rome documents rather than left to the authorities in Maputo. He wanted a stipulation that the new assembly would as its first act either ratify or amend the current constitution, which had been adopted by the one-party state. Raffaelli suggested that it would be better to leave to the new assembly the power to decide on its own agenda.

From December 10 to 15 RENAMO held its second party congress at its headquarters in Gorongosa.[4] This meeting marked a further step in the process of transformation of RENAMO from a military insurgency to a political party—a transformation that was essential for the overall success of the peace process. The RENAMO congress re-elected Dhlakama president and authorized several changes to strengthen the civilian structure at headquarters. In a news conference after the congress, Dhlakama said, "The congress decided that the peace talks are the only solution, the only way to attain real peace, democracy, freedom, and justice."[5] The RENAMO delegation departed for Rome before the congress concluded.

Irrespective of a formal decision to invite additional governments to join the talks, Washington knew that both parties and the mediators would welcome a U.S. technical team at the resumed talks in December. The U.S. team included a military adviser (Lieutenant Colonel Charles Snyder), a lawyer (John Byerly), and the Mozambique desk officer (William Jackson). The team planned to meet separately with the mediators and the parties to share ideas, provide technical advice, and promote solutions.

On December 16 Zuppi met with the U.S. team. He expected the talks to last only four days. Because this was not enough time to resolve differences on specific issues such as the constitutional requirement of majority elections and RENAMO's demand for proportional representation, the mediators decided to aim for an agreement on general principles for the election law, such as freedom of expression and association. While working on a statement of principles, the mediators intended to draw out the views of both parties on specific issues—information that the mediators could then use to prepare a redraft of the election law protocol before talks resumed in January. After an initial plenary meeting, the mediators expected to facilitate the talks by shuttling between the two delegations.

Zuppi said the mediators intended to press for a two-week Christmas cease-fire. Because there had been problems in verifying compliance with the December 1 agreement and no mechanism existed to monitor a cease-fire throughout the country, the mediators feared that an unverified cease-fire more than two weeks long could lead to recriminations over cease-fire violations and thereby discredit the peace process. The mediators did not expect the parties to resolve during the next few days their differences regarding which additional governments to invite to the talks.

For the time being the mediators, who thought that the formal structure for the talks should not be changed until the protocol on election law was completed, did not intend to take any initiative on this issue.

The government delegation preferred that the protocol on election law simply state the principles on which the government would then draft the actual legislative proposal for submission to the assembly. The few days before the planned interval for the Christmas holidays could best be used to elicit RENAMO positions on the election law. As for the proposed Christmas cease-fire, the government wanted a one-month cease-fire that would be in effect until talks resumed in January. The government delegation expected that the JVC could monitor the cease-fire, but it had not raised this possibility with members of the JVC or worked out its own plan for the JVC monitoring. Unlike the mediators, the government delegation expressed no concern over the possible negative consequences of a prolonged, unmonitored cease-fire.

After the RENAMO delegation returned to Rome on December 17, the mediators hosted two plenary sessions the next day to discuss the election system. The government and RENAMO delegations agreed that the elections for president and national assembly should be held simultaneously and that a period of twelve months from cease-fire to elections would be adequate. Guebuza explained that the government would insist on a majority election system (implying but not requiring one-member constituencies in which the leading candidate won); Domingos said RENAMO wanted a proportional system, with ten constituencies. Although he never explained in detail why RENAMO preferred this system, one reason must have been simply an understandable desire not to accept the government's own proposal for a majority election system.

The constant conflict over legitimacy was exemplified by RENAMO's demand for an explicit agreement that the new assembly's first order of business be to review the constitution. After the assembly had completed this review, the new president could be installed. Despite the provision in the constitution requiring a qualified majority of two-thirds for constitutional amendments, RENAMO assumed that the new assembly would have the power to change the constitution with a simple majority vote.

The government insisted that Protocol I, accepted and signed by RENAMO, had removed from the negotiating table any claim to change the constitution. It objected to any delay in the installation of the new president, explaining that a vacuum of power would be harmful to the peace process. The government assumed that a two-thirds majority, as required by the constitution in force, would be needed to amend the constitution.

RENAMO wanted the United Nations to conduct the elections, but the government objected that this would be a violation of national sovereignty. The government did not want any intrusive UN role, nor did it want to share with RENAMO any responsibility for administering the elections.

While the mediators were working on the election issues, the U.S. team probed the two sides for views on a Christmas cease-fire. Achieving a cease-fire would be a positive step, if both sides kept to its terms. The U.S. team used its meetings to prod both sides to consider how to arrange and manage a cease-fire. Neither side had given this problem detailed thought, and these technical discussions introduced concepts that would come back into play when negotiations reached the agenda item on a cease-fire. Domingos feared that the government would take advantage of a Christmas cease-fire to resupply its troops and that inadequate arrangements for verification would put RENAMO at a severe disadvantage. For this reason the U.S. team suggested that any cease-fire be for no more than two weeks, the length of RENAMO's unilateral cease-fire the previous Christmas. To avoid the complications of drafting a joint statement, the Christmas cease-fire could be based on unilateral commitments to the mediators.

On December 20 the two parties and the mediators issued a joint communique. In it they recorded agreement to hold the elections for president and assembly at the same time, to conduct the elections within a year of a general peace agreement, and to involve both the United Nations and the Organization of African Unity (OAU) in the election process. There was no agreement on a Christmas cease-fire, nor mention of any specific issues yet to resolve. The parties announced their intention to resume negotiations on January 15, 1992.

During the four days of meetings, the issue of inviting additional governments to participate in the talks had not been raised. Without any formal status the U.S. team had been able to work with the mediators and both delegations, an arrangement that was acceptable for the time being to all concerned.

On December 21 Dhlakama told a press conference that RENAMO would insist on a suspension of certain articles of the constitution before elections. "The constitution must be revised before we sign the cease-fire accord. We must indicate which of its articles and laws must be suspended. . . . It is up to RENAMO to point out certain articles that it perceives as dangerous to any electoral process in our country."[6]

Round Nine Resumed: January 20 to February 15, 1992

In January 1992 President Chissano asked President Mugabe to meet with Dhlakama to sound out RENAMO's leader on the idea of preparing for a summit.[7] Once again LONRHO's Tiny Rowland, who had helped arrange the aborted negotiations in Malawi in June 1990, promoted the meeting between Mugabe and Dhlakama, and President Hastings Kamuzu Banda of Malawi was the host. Dhlakama still accepted LONRHO's material assistance and organizational support for making such arrangements. The venue and list of participants for this meeting were a reminder that the war in Mozambique had significant regional consequences involving the interests of neighboring states. On the evening of January 9 there were initial contacts, and Dhlakama sought unsuccessfully to get endorsement of his request for a summit meeting with President Chissano. Then Banda, Mugabe, and Dhlakama met at noon the next day and agreed on the aim of ending the war and securing the withdrawal of all foreign troops.[8]

The U.S. technical team of Snyder, Byerly, and Jackson returned to Rome in mid-January. Byerly and Jackson planned to consult with the parties separately and with the mediators in such a way as to supplement the mediators' efforts on the election law protocol. Snyder had a different role. Taking into account the difficulties that surfaced during the negotiations over a possible Christmas cease-fire, he returned to help the parties prepare to negotiate arrangements for a cease-fire.

Snyder gave both sides a paper outlining the four phases of a cease-fire operation and detailing the steps to be taken in each phase. Phase one begins with the signing of the cease-fire document and the arrival of international observers: hostilities stop, field commanders set up liaison links and share information with the cease-fire commission, and cease-fire observers arrive in country. Phase two begins when the cease-fire comes officially into force; it should take about one week for the observers to move into field locations. Phase three involves movement of combatant military forces to sites identified for cantonment; this operation could take a month. Phase four consists of the full operation of the cease-fire commission, demobilization of forces, and creation of the new national army. Snyder attached to this outline a brief questionnaire to focus the parties' attention on key decisions to be made in designing the details of a cease-fire.

During the month since Christmas, none of the difficult issues had become easier. Both delegations returned to the negotiating table with written proposals. The government wanted the third protocol to contain only general principles for drafting the election law because the power to draft legislation belonged to the government and the power to enact laws belonged to the assembly in Maputo. RENAMO wanted the protocol to contain detailed provisions covering all aspects of the new election system, and it included in its text one provision to suspend after a cease-fire the "state of emergency" powers that the present constitution granted to President Chissano and a second provision to provide RENAMO with logistical and financial support for its launch as a political party. RENAMO pressed for a commitment that the new assembly's first order of business would be constitutional reform.

During the first plenary session on January 21, Domingos presented RENAMO's draft. This document was five pages long in single-spaced text, and the first three pages consisted of sections on freedom of the press and access to the mass media, on freedom of association and expression, on freedom of movement and domicile, and on the return and reintegration of refugees and displaced persons. The one-page description of "a democratic, impartial, and pluralistic electoral system" contained the qualifications for voting and for being a candidate to office, an outline of a system of proportional representation for assembly elections, a requirement that the president be chosen by direct majority vote, limitations on electoral coalitions among parties, and provision for the state to subsidize the election campaigns of parties and to provide lodging and other facilities for RENAMO "in all the provincial and district capitals and other localities in the country." The final page of RENAMO's draft described how a UN operation should be established to facilitate, monitor, and verify the elections.

On January 24 the government made its counterproposal, which was only half as long as the RENAMO draft. The RENAMO draft contained elements the government could accept, Guebuza explained, "but it also contains several points that we consider unclear, controversial, or even unacceptable, on which we must concentrate efforts to achieve clarity and consensus." The government's draft stated, "The electoral law, to be drafted by the Government in consultation with all political parties legally established in the country, will indicate the characteristics, modalities, and circumstances for conducting general elections." The system for elections to the national assembly would be "in harmony with the principle of proportional representation." A candidate for president would have to win 50 percent of the vote to be elected; if need be, a runoff election between the two leading candidates would be held. Brief sections followed on foreign observers, freedom of the press and access to the mass media, freedom of association and expression, freedom of movement, return and reintegration of refugees and displaced persons, and a donors conference.

At this point Domingos asked the mediators to prepare a "side-by-side" text matching the comparable parts of the two proposals. Although in some circumstances a side-by-side text can facilitate negotiations by identifying points of convergence and divergence, this method often accentuates the elements of conflict that the presence of a mediator tends to restrain. It diminishes the mediator's ability to lead the negotiating process by producing a mediator's single text and using that to elicit the positions of the parties.

The side-by-side text followed the order of RENAMO's proposal, making it immediately apparent that the government's proposal contained much shorter provisions on freedom of the press, freedom of speech and association, freedom of movement, and the right of refugees and displaced persons to return to their homes. On these issues at least there was no direct conflict between the two versions. Both versions recommended that election to the assembly be based on a system of proportional representation and that the president be elected by direct vote, but RENAMO's draft had additional requirements: For a party to win any seats in an electoral district, it would have to win 20 percent of the vote; a candidate for president would have to be nominated by a petition with at least 100,000 signatures; and there would be public funding for election campaigns. Both drafts included a role for UN and OAU election observers, but RENAMO's draft added a provision for an election commission with RENAMO membership. The government's draft had no provision on constitutional review, a critical issue for RENAMO.

With encouragement from the U.S. observers, the mediators began to prepare a mediators' single text including those elements on which the two sides were not so far apart. After an initial round of contacts but before drafting began, the mediators already saw conflicts on several issues in sharp focus: RENAMO wanted an independent election commission to be responsible for the conduct of the elections, but the government insisted on conducting the elections itself. RENAMO wanted a requirement that a party receive at least 20 percent of the vote before gaining representation in the Assembly of the Republic, but the government insisted that this barrier be no higher than 4 percent. RENAMO wanted the minimum age for members of the assembly set at twenty-five, the government suggested eighteen. RENAMO set the number of signatures on nominating petitions for president at 100,000, but the government wanted it no higher than several thousand. The government wanted a runoff in the presidential election if no candidate received 50 percent of the vote, but RENAMO wanted no runoff unless the top two candidates received exactly the same number of votes. Finally, RENAMO wanted a compulsory review of the constitution by the assembly as its first item of business, but the government rejected compulsory review.

From Saturday, January 25, to Wednesday, January 29, the State Department's experts worked with a staff member of the Community of Sant'Egidio to produce a single text that the mediators could put forward. To expedite the process of drafting, the U.S. experts met separately with both delegations, coordinated with the mediators, and then revised the draft language to conform to the substantive positions of both sides wherever possible. In a few places, such as the dispute over how many signatures were needed on a petition to nominate a candidate for president, the draft left a blank to be filled in later. The mediators then reviewed this text, adjusted it in line with what they had learned during their own discussions with the parties, and prepared to present it on January 31. Regarding the constitution, this draft stated simply that each party represented in the new assembly would have the right to submit draft amendments that would have to be considered by the assembly.

On January 30 Dhlakama held another press conference. After reviewing the differences between the drafts proposed by RENAMO and the government, he again voiced RENAMO's objection to the constitution. "That is not a Mozambican constitution. It is a FRELIMO constitution. One cannot transform a party document into a national constitution. A constitution is a document drafted and ratified by a democratically elected assembly where people have the capacity to deal with constitutional matters and have the interests of the Mozambican people at heart."[9] Dhlakama insisted that his concern with the constitution be kept on the negotiating table at all times.

On January 31 Ambassador Davidow, who was en route to southern Africa with the team that had worked on the Angola negotiations, stopped in Rome to meet with the mediators and separately with the government and RENAMO delegations. Earlier in the morning the mediators had presented their proposed draft to both parties during a plenary session. At a working lunch Davidow and his delegation met with the mediators, who gave a synopsis of the status of the negotiations. Without going into the issues at stake in the text before the parties, Davidow said the United States supported the mediators' work. Looking to the future, how did the mediators expect to bring other governments into the negotiations as observers when discussion of the military issues began? Did they have any means for responding to RENAMO's pleas for assistance in becoming a political party?

Raffaelli said the observer issue should be resolved before military talks began. Within two weeks Portugal's Durao Barroso was expected in Rome, and his visit would be an occasion to discuss this issue. Two more weeks might be required to conclude the protocol on the election system. Then there might be a week before military talks began, and if the two parties kept to the pace, a peace accord could be finished by the end of June. As for support for RENAMO, the mediators' draft contained a provision requiring the government to make office facilities available to RENAMO, and the Italian Parliament had just authorized the government to use up to one percent of its foreign aid budget to support a peace process. Some of this money could be used to set up RENAMO as a political party.

Davidow later met with the delegations of the parties. Each reviewed its position on the issues in the protocol and expressed appreciation for the support that the United States was giving the negotiating process. Guebuza emphasized that the draft must not cast doubt on the legitimacy of the constitution; Domingos insisted that the draft must explicitly provide for the new assembly to review the constitution. Domingos repeated that RENAMO needed financial support to operate as a political party and that a visit by Dhlakama to the United States was needed to overcome the negative image created by the Gersony report. Davidow responded that the U.S. government did not have funds for direct support to a political party and that a cease-fire would create more favorable circumstances for a U.S. visit by Dhlakama.

After Davidow's visit, the mediators kept up their method of consulting separately with each party and then amending their draft. On February 4 they presented a slightly revised version to both parties. On February 6 the government presented a counterproposal, which involved eliminating more than 25 percent of the draft. As for the constitution, it included this provision: "In accordance with the constitution, the assembly of the republic will have the authority to determine its own agenda, including the power to consider any proposals to amend the constitution."

On leaving Rome, Davidow continued his trip to Angola and South Africa. The peace process in Angola, despite difficulties, was going forward; it was natural to hope that progress there would encourage both parties in the Rome talks. The South Africans thought that more international exposure would help Dhlakama overcome his distrust of the negotiating process. Dhlakama's January meeting with Mugabe had helped;

a summit with Chissano would do even more. Although the South Africans had interests at stake in the Mozambique peace process, they were now willing to wait on the sidelines rather than claim any direct role for themselves.

On February 7 Davidow met with President Chissano in Maputo. Chissano objected to RENAMO's insistence that the government agree in advance that the next assembly review the constitution as its first order of business. The assembly could amend the constitution, but Chissano did not want the Rome negotiating process to compel the assembly to do so.

Given the constant recurrence of this dispute, it appeared that the compromise language of Protocol I had not settled the problem of legitimacy. Both sides wanted to go into an election campaign with their own spin on the constitutional issue: the government that it had brought democracy to Mozambique, and RENAMO that the multiparty election it had fought for could create the basis for a democratic constitution. If this dispute could not be resolved now, perhaps it could be postponed for resolution later. To reach an early agreement on the election law protocol, the mediators could propose lifting the constitutional issue out of the negotiations at this point for assured consideration later. Given the structure of the May 28 agenda, one logical place to return to this issue would be under the item on guarantees, which would be reached after the items on military issues and a cease-fire.

On February 10 Davidow, then in Harare, discussed the Mozambique peace process with President Mugabe. This meeting was an opportunity to discuss how to build regional involvement in the peace process, as Mugabe had done a month earlier through his meeting with Dhlakama in Malawi. Zimbabwe had real interests and involvement in this issue; Mugabe now had contact with both sides; and more than any other state in the region, Zimbabwe could help move both parties toward a settlement. Could a way be found to do this within the framework of the ongoing talks in Rome?

The next day Davidow met Dhlakama in Lilongwe. According to a communique issued by RENAMO,[10] Dhlakama reviewed the status of the talks, emphasizing that the current Mozambican constitution was undemocratic. RENAMO did not demand that a new constitution be put in place before elections, but it insisted that as a condition for holding elections those articles of the constitution that granted extraordinary powers to the president be suspended. Dhlakama discussed RENAMO's views on the number of signatures needed to nominate a presidential candidate, a national election commission, and the system for electing the president. Davidow emphasized that the way to resolve these concerns was to go ahead in the negotiations. If agreement were reached, the involvement of the international community was the best guarantee that the government would have to conduct the elections by democratic standards and not threaten RENAMO and its leaders with use of force.

Round Nine Concluded: February 12 to March 12, 1992

On February 12 Italian foreign minister de Michelis and Portuguese secretary of state Durao Barroso discussed what formal arrangement might be used to bring other governments into the negotiating process. In speaking to the press after the meeting, Durao Barroso said that Portugal supported the Rome negotiating process. De Michelis said Italy welcomed Portuguese support and looked forward to Portugal's joining the process as an official observer. Ignoring the instrumental role played by Mario Raffaelli and his own ministry in support of the talks, de Michelis suggested that Italy should also join the talks as an official observer. This statement created confusion among the Mozambicans, who knew that the Italian government had already taken on responsibility for the talks in a real if indirect way by underwriting the negotiations hosted at Sant'Egidio's headquarters.

After Davidow's talks with Chissano and Dhlakama, the mediators proposed to Guebuza and Domingos that they defer the issue of the constitution. On February 13 Guebuza told U.S. observer Hume that a compromise could be found to resolve all the issues on the table except for RENAMO's insistence that the first business of the new assembly be to confirm or amend the constitution. Guebuza said that deferral in a neutral form might be one way around this impasse.

Domingos was skeptical about the merits of deferral. RENAMO, given its fifteen-year experience with FRELIMO rule, did not trust FRELIMO or its constitution. Domingos was convinced that the new assembly would have to review the existing constitution to produce a true multiparty constitution. Hume suggested that an agreed deferral until the item on guarantees could give RENAMO more leverage on this issue. The government would already have conceded that the issue was on the table; because arrangements for a cease-fire would have been agreed to at that point, the government would have more reason to be flexible; and the inclusion of other governments as observers would give more weight to any commitments made. Domingos responded that he would reflect on these points.

By February 20 the mediators, by meeting first with one negotiating team and then with the other, were moving the parties toward solutions on the share of the vote required for a party to receive seats in the assembly, the number of signatures required to nominate a presidential candidate, and the age requirement for members of the assembly. The blanks in the mediators' text were being filled in. The minimum for representation in the assembly would be between 5 and 20 percent of the votes cast in a constituency; 10,000 signatures would be needed to nominate a candidate for president; the president would be elected by an absolute majority of votes cast, with a runoff election if need be. Domingos had agreed that the issue of the constitution could be deferred, but there was not yet agreement on the form in which deferral would be accomplished.

To prepare the ground for military discussions, which would involve more participants, the U.S. observer explored with the parties and the mediators options for organizing the next round of talks. The mediators and both delegations expected to invite other governments—probably the United States and Portugal and possibly the United Kingdom and France—to join the talks as official observers. The delegations that had so far conducted the talks would be reinforced by teams of military experts. One possibility was for the military teams to form a working group with military experts from observer delegations to explore options; the working group's product could be forwarded to the heads of delegation for further evaluation, negotiation, and decision. Observers might not be present for meetings at the level of heads of delegation. A working group format might foster collaboration by avoiding the formality of plenary sessions and by removing the separation that the mediators' use of bilateral consultations had permitted so far. The Italian government was willing to provide one sequestered site for the next round, so that social mingling and concentration of effort could create additional momentum for the peace process.

Meanwhile the worsening drought throughout southern Africa was bringing another disaster to Mozambique, and humanitarian assistance agencies feared widespread starvation in the countryside before the year ended. On February 18 a Voice of RENAMO radio broadcast criticized relief agencies in Mozambique for not delivering assistance in RENAMO-controlled areas.[11] In fact relief agencies had not been so active in RENAMO-controlled areas primarily because they could not get adequate access and security for their operations. The ICRC had long faced this difficulty, despite its repeated contacts with RENAMO officials. Until this time RENAMO had given low priority to the problem of humanitarian relief, and the FAM did not favor expediting the delivery of supplies that could help RENAMO forces. Both sides had learned to live with the military stalemate, but perhaps the dire need for relief supplies throughout the country, including in RENAMO controlled areas, could finally give a sense of urgency to the negotiations.

On March 3 and 4 the mediators held two long sessions with Guebuza and Domingos to go over their text line by line. The substantive differences were being narrowed down to the classical issue of jobs and money: how the members of the national election commission would be chosen and how election campaign funds would be managed and distributed.

Dhlakama arrived in Rome on March 4, and solutions to all outstanding issues were quickly found.

A week later, on March 12, Protocol III, on the election law, was signed at Sant'Egidio by the heads of delegation and the mediators. To register their agreement to defer the issue of the constitution, at the same time they signed an "agreed note" that stated that "they identified the continuation of differences relating to the relationship between a new Assembly of the Republic, the actual Constitution and the procedures for eventual modifications of the same, and the parties agreed, as proposed by the mediators, to postpone the discussion of this point to a time that will be determined by the mediators in consultation with the parties."

Before Dhlakama departed Rome, Hume informed him that the U.S. government would welcome two of his collaborators in Washington to discuss items on the Rome agenda before the resumption of talks, planned for early April. Dhlakama was delighted, but he decided not to send any of his subordinates on a trip he preferred to make himself.

It was striking how little direct interaction there had been so far between the government and RENAMO negotiating teams. The procedure of meeting together only in formal sessions with the mediators present and then maintaining a dialogue only through the mediators compensated for the distrust between the parties. However, this procedure did not encourage the parties to build trust by working together directly. To achieve reconciliation, the overall goal of the peace process, the parties would eventually have to learn to work together without the constant involvement of the mediators.

Dhlakama was worried about securing the wherewithal to change RENAMO from a rural insurgency into a political party. In mid-March he wrote to Raffaelli, as representative of the Italian government and lead mediator, to say that RENAMO needed a concrete guarantee of outside financial support. Italy was giving millions of dollars to FRELIMO, so why could it not give 10 or 12 million to RENAMO?[12] However inelegant Dhlakama's solicitation, the need he expressed was genuine. For peace to take hold, RENAMO would need help for its transformation into a civilian political party.

The character of the negotiations was about to change. Until this point, the agenda items discussed had been relatively abstract political questions, and the agreements reached would be implemented toward the end of the peace process, one year after a cease-fire began the transition period. The remaining agenda items were relatively concrete military and administrative questions, and implementation of agreements on these items would have to begin on the day of a cease-fire. From here on, the stakes would be higher and the effects more immediate.

Two important elements of reality had not yet found expression in the negotiating process. Mass starvation threatened the Mozambican people because the drought in southern Africa had destroyed another year's crops and because the war impeded delivery of relief supplies. Could this element of *force majeure* create a sense of urgency to push the parties toward peace? Because neighboring states also suffered from the drought and depended on Mozambique's transport lines, they too had a strong interest in ending the war.

The Mozambican parties and the mediators had assumed that the international community would have many tasks to perform in implementing the peace agreement: monitoring a cease-fire, helping to form a new national army, repatriating refugees, resettling displaced persons, providing relief supplies and development aid, and monitoring elections. So far the international community had not participated in the talks. If representatives of several governments and the United Nations participated in the negotiations, the international community would be in a better position to provide the resources needed for implementation. The peace process would undergo a qualitative change when the parties signed their final agreements and had to begin implementation. Could international participation now help prepare for that change?

five

Expanding the Framework

Mediators can change the rules. Most simply and drastically they do so by abandoning the parties to resolve their dispute by themselves. Alternatively, mediators can change the character of their facilitation—for example, by insisting that drafts be prepared in joint working groups, not just reviewed by heads of delegation in separate consultions with the mediators. In some negotiations, mediators control the agenda and therefore can rearrange the order of work or set deadlines. Mediators can change the number of participants, perhaps bringing in more parties to have additional interests represented at the table. A mediator would normally seek the consent of the parties before making such changes.

Up to this point the low-profile, non-diplomatic status of the mediation had made it easier to convene talks and offered maximum flexibility for facilitating dialogue. The mediators had gradually coaxed the parties forward through the explicitly political items on the agenda. But such low-profile mediation had no leverage over the parties, no power to confer diplomatic legitimacy on any agreement, and very little capacity to sustain the process of implementation that was being designed at the negotiating table.

The next round of talks had to deal with the military items and arrangements for implementation. The mediators would need technical advice on these subjects from governments or the United Nations. If the United Nations became involved in the talks, UN standard operating procedures could be a guideline for designing the mechanism for implementing the agreements. The parties, who so far had needed only to satisfy each other, would then have to meet UN requirements if the United

Nations were to have a central role in the implementation. Bringing the international community into the talks would strengthen the negotiating framework, pushing the parties toward practical solutions.

So far the negotiations had directly involved the parties and the mediation team. What relationship could the observers from other governments have to the negotiations? These additional players could support the mediation and the agreement that emerged, or they could seek to replace the mediation and oppose the emerging agreement. Another option, to endorse the mediation but to object to some of its results, would be a contradiction in fact. This option, even if objections were framed in terms of merely seeking necessary improvements, could only delegitimize both the mediation and its results.

The government and RENAMO had begun their dialogue after the long military stalemate had deprived both sides of the illusion that they could prevail by force of arms. There was no support either from the superpowers or from neighboring states for continuing the war, and the parties had been advised to negotiate its end. The humanitarian crisis facing the country was gradually creating a sense of urgency.

Preparing the Next Phase: March 15 to June 9, 1992

The participants considered four changes in the structure of the negotiations. With the shift to military issues, delegations would for the first time have to include military experts, and the mediation based at Sant'Egidio would need help from Italian government experts to guide the discussions. The pending issue of bringing in additional governments as observers would have to be resolved. The worsening drought made the issue of humanitarian relief, which the ICRC had raised at the time the talks began in July 1990, too acute for the negotiators to ignore. Finally, Chissano and Dhlakama were exploring the possibility of a summit meeting.

To make plans for discussion of military issues, Deputy Assistant Secretary Davidow met in Rome with the mediators and with Under Secretary Bruno Bottai at the Italian Foreign Ministry on March 26 and 27. Some changes in the structure of the talks now seemed inevitable: a more prominent role for the Italian government through the involvement of its military experts, an increase in the size of the parties' delegations to include military teams, and a role for military experts from the governments to be invited as observers. Davidow referred to the experience of the Angola negotiations and suggested there were other steps to consider: whether to move the talks to a new site where the participants could be sequestered and the pace of work more continuous; whether the pattern of infrequent formal plenary sessions supplemented by the mediators' bilateral consultations with each delegation could be replaced by establishment of informal working groups to explore options and prepare documents for decision by heads of delegation; whether the Italian Foreign Ministry should set up a small secretariat to help manage the talks and coordinate the involvement of the observer delegations; and which governments should be invited to become observers and exactly what role they could play.

The next week, U.S. legal and military experts were in Rome to discuss the same questions. In a meeting with Italian experts, both sides recognized that it would be a challenge to make the physical arrangements for a monitored cease-fire in a country the size of Mozambique, in which there was no clear front line and only rudimentary infrastructure.

By the end of March, the drought throughout southern Africa made it certain that a major food relief effort would be required in the coming months. Mozambique's per capita gross national product had fallen to eighty dollars a year; the comparable figure for Somalia, then suffering mass starvation, was half again as high. The situation in Mozambique was critical because of the number of displaced persons in the country and because of the country's importance as a transshipment point for food moving inland to Malawi and Zimbabwe. Addressing either of these needs would require arrangements with the combatants. Although in the past such arrangements had proved impossible, the lack of food was putting pressure on both combatants—particularly RENAMO, which had previously supplied itself by foraging and pillaging civilian supplies. The ICRC had put forward three proposals for the concurrence of both parties: first, that some areas (especially near the border with Malawi, where large numbers of displaced persons congregated) be declared safe areas; second, that the parties permit the ICRC to conduct cross-border operations to supply such areas; and third, because the volume of food aid required could no longer be provided by airlift, that a limited number of roads be opened to bring food into the hinterland.

The drought was creating some sense of urgency. Both parties felt the immediate effect of declining food supplies. Malawi and Zimbabwe, both suffering from food shortages, depended on supplies coming in overland across Mozambique and feared a further exodus of Mozambican refugees into their countries. The donor community, already providing more than $1 billion a year in aid to Mozambique, was aware that unless a cease-fire was reached it would be impossible to deliver to the rural population the volume of food aid required before the next harvest at the end of the year. Until this point, because of the justifiable concern that humanitarian relief not be used as a political lever, the issue had not been incorporated into the negotiations in Rome. Could the mediators now harness the sense of urgency caused by the drought to make progress at the negotiating table?

At the end of March, Dhlakama broadcast on the Voice of RENAMO a demand for a summit with President Chissano. Two months had passed since he and President Mugabe had discussed the possibility, and now he decided to go public:

> I would like to propose that President Chissano and I, Afonso Dhlakama, should travel to Rome at the next round of talks so that the two of us will negotiate peace face to face. It would be the two leaders. Instead of Guebuza and Raul [Domingos], it will be Dhlakama and Chissano, [meeting] face to face to negotiate. Furthermore, I would also like to propose that a cease-fire should be declared in a matter of weeks rather than two or three months. We could cease fire within four weeks. We could agree on a cease-fire, and then we could continue to negotiate with a cease-fire in place. Here at home there are 150 humanitarian organizations which have only been working on the side of FRELIMO. Those organizations would be officially allowed to operate in all areas of the country.

At the beginning of April, RENAMO's national council met to consider its positions for the peace talks. Its final communique insisted that FRELIMO "agree to discuss the constitution in order to suspend all the articles which jeopardize the democratization process; FRELIMO must agree that the assembly elected in the elections should review this constitution."[1] In other points the communique called for a unified national army of less than 23,000 troops; those FRELIMO and RENAMO troops not enrolled in the new army would be demobilized and reintegrated into society. The police and state security services would have to be restructured, and RENAMO members would join these forces. During the period between the cease-fire and elections, UN teams would monitor the situation inside the country, refugees would return for resettlement, political prisoners would be freed, and all parties would gain access to the news media. In derogation of the obligation in Protocol I of October 18 to accept the government's administration of the country after a cease-fire, the communique stated that "after the signing of a cease-fire agreement, the southern territory under RENAMO control should continue to be under its control as a way of avoiding misunderstandings with

FRELIMO."[2] The communique ended with criticism of western governments, especially the United States, for not welcoming RENAMO officials and not supporting RENAMO.

On April 9 the Italian ambassador in Maputo, Manfredo Incisa di Camerana, sent a cable to Rome pointing out that the consequences of the drought were becoming dramatic. The government, because of humanitarian aid from the international community, could feed people in the territory under its control; hungry people from RENAMO-controlled areas were migrating toward the government's food distribution centers. RENAMO could get food by raiding the centers, but such action would cause it to lose any credibility it had gained at the negotiating table. Alternatively, RENAMO would have to play for an early cease-fire that would permit more food distribution in RENAMO-controlled areas. The cable concluded, "Dhlakama knows the only solution would be agreement for a cease-fire."[3]

On April 15 Assistant Secretary Cohen, who had been on another visit to Angola, arrived in Maputo. He met with President Chissano the next day. They discussed how to create more momentum for the peace talks in Rome. Cohen wondered whether a Chissano-Dhlakama summit could be used to arrange a truce to enable international humanitarian agencies to move food inland by road and to set a target date, perhaps three months in advance, for completion of the Rome talks. Chissano said that both the meeting between President Mugabe and Dhlakama in January and a later contact between Foreign Minister Mocumbi and Jose Castro, a senior RENAMO official, had explored the possibility of a summit. The obstacles were that RENAMO had refused preliminary meetings, a specific agenda, and adequate preparation. It was important to plan how a summit would relate to the Rome talks and how a truce would be monitored.

Cohen said the United States supported the Rome talks as the main element in the peace process. Additional governments should be involved when military issues and implementation were discussed. He encouraged Chissano to pursue the idea of a well-prepared summit to arrange a truce so that roads could be opened for the distribution of relief supplies, to address guarantees for the transitional period, and to set a date by which the negotiators should complete their work on a peace accord. Chissano said he would welcome a summit, on the condition that it was well prepared.

The next day, April 17, the Voice of RENAMO broadcast a statement that "Afonso Dhlakama, the father of democracy in Mozambique, is willing to meet Herman Cohen in order to brief him on the political situation in Mozambique, and the responsibilities that ought to be assumed so that peace may be attained in Mozambique."[4]

On April 25 Cohen met with Dhlakama in Lilongwe. After reiterating U.S. support for the Rome peace process, Cohen pointed out that because the drought now threatened mass starvation in the Mozambican countryside, a new sense of urgency was needed to establish conditions for delivery of relief supplies. At a well-prepared summit, Dhlakama and Chissano might announce a target date for completion of the negotiations, arrange a three-month truce or at least open transport corridors throughout the country to permit delivery of humanitarian assistance, and overcome differences between the guarantees to be agreed to in Rome and the provisions of the constitution.

Dhlakama now showed no desire for a summit with President Chissano and admitted to no sense of urgency regarding the delivery of humanitarian assistance. The Rome talks could resume to discuss military issues. He repeated the criticism of the constitution that was contained in the communique issued in early April by RENAMO's national council, insisting that these problems be discussed and resolved before a peace accord could be signed. He was skeptical that a temporary truce could be made to work; when the government had violated the December 1 agreement, the verification commission had not acted. How would a three-month truce be monitored? The United Nations would have to be brought in to verify any final cease-fire. He doubted that transport corridors for food could work and suggested that humanitarian agencies use planes to deliver food inland. Looking toward the completion of the Rome peace process, Dhlakama said RENAMO needed such resources as offices, housing, cars, equipment, and money to prepare its people for civilian life. Governments that supported the negotiations and might help implement a settlement should welcome him in their capitals.

During the meeting, Cohen seemed to persuade Dhlakama on some points. Dhlakama agreed to the release of a joint press statement indicating that he "withdrew his previous positions that the talks should first address constitutional issues and agreed to proceed with discussion of military issues, leaving RENAMO's constitutional and transitional concerns to be addressed under agenda item number five on guarantees." The statement announced a change in Dhlakama's position on expediting delivery of humanitarian relief supplies. "President Dhlakama and Assistant Secretary Cohen agreed on the urgency of assuring adequate drought relief to all Mozambicans as well as guarantees for the safe delivery of food supplies to Mozambique's drought-stricken neighbors. They agreed that it would be desirable to establish corridors or other means of delivering relief supplies while providing adequate guarantees that these arrangements would not be exploited for military advantage."[5]

Despite Cohen's efforts, the parties still did not act with any sense of immediate urgency.

One month later, Ambassador Incisa traveled to Gorongosa to talk with Dhlakama. Incisa's first tack was to probe Dhlakama's thinking on a possible summit, and he presented a draft that the two leaders could use as the basis for a summit declaration. Its main points were a truce for a period to be specified, supervision of the truce by the JVC, facilitation by the government and by RENAMO of the delivery of relief supplies, reconvening of the Rome negotiations so that the remaining protocols would be completed by a specific date, and agreement that "any divergence in the views remaining between the parties regarding the relationship between the assembly of the republic to be elected and the constitution currently in effect will be discussed under the point on the agenda regarding guarantees." As he had in his meeting with Cohen, Dhlakama showed little interest in a summit.

Incisa then turned to the prospects for the tenth round of peace talks. Dhlakama, who had recently returned from a visit to London and was planning one to Paris, now accepted the government's proposal to invite France, Portugal, the United Kingdom, and the United States to send observers to the talks. The observers could participate fully in technical discussions of military issues and would be allowed to attend formal plenary sessions, but they should be excluded from meetings with heads of delegation on political questions. Dhlakama showed no interest in opening corridors to speed relief supplies or in an early summit with Chissano. He did agree, however, that the Catholic charity Caritas could bring relief supplies by air into some RENAMO-controlled areas, including Gorongosa. He would authorize his delegation in Rome to deal with the issue of humanitarian relief, perhaps proposing an international committee including the United Nations, the ICRC, interested governments, and humanitarian relief agencies as members to coordinate and monitor relief operations throughout Mozambique.

The next week, on May 31 and June 1, Deputy Assistant Secretary Davidow represented the United States in Geneva at a UN pledging conference for humanitarian assistance to countries affected by the drought in southern Africa, including Mozambique. He announced a U.S. pledge of $285 million, which would consist mostly of more than one million metric tons of food aid. After the Geneva conference, Davidow came to Rome to consult briefly with the mediators and the Italian government on plans to resume the Rome negotiations.

Round Ten Starts: June 10 to July 1, 1992

Dhlakama's spokesman issued a communique in Gorongosa on June 9 to announce positions that RENAMO's delegation would take back to Rome. In addition to points on the constitution, army, and security service already contained in the national council statement issued at the beginning of April, this document called on the delegations in Rome to authorize humanitarian assistance agencies in Mozambique to deliver help to the entire population, including the people in areas under RENAMO control.[6] This help would have to be delivered by airplane in some areas, the communique insisted, because the government would take advantage of opened roads to launch military offensives against RENAMO.

At the June 10 plenary session that opened the tenth round of talks, both Mozambican delegations approved an invitation from the mediators to the governments of France, Portugal, the United Kingdom, and the United States, as well as to the United Nations, to send representatives to observe the talks. The mediators' letter to those governments explained that the observers could participate in meetings on both military and political issues; to preserve the direct dialogue between the parties, the observers' contributions should be expressed "at the margins of the meetings." The mediators indicated there would be periodic meetings at the Italian Foreign Ministry to permit the mediators and observers to exchange views and coordinate efforts. The first such meeting took place two days later.

For the next week and a half the mediators conducted bilateral sessions with both sides to resolve the issue postponed from round nine: when to discuss the issue of the constitution. After arduous efforts with both sides, the mediators made progress with a three-part solution: first, to add to the item on guarantees in the May 28, 1991, agenda a subitem entitled "constitutional questions"; second, to reorder the agenda so that guarantees would be discussed between military questions and a cease-fire; third, to consider these three items "as parts of a whole and, once agreement is reached on each point, to initial the respective protocols, which will be signed together as rapidly as possible."[7] For the first time, the parties had apparently given the mediators the flexibility to prepare a package deal.

France, Portugal, the United Kingdom, and the United States quickly accepted the invitation to send observers, and on June 18 Secretary-General

Boutros Boutros-Ghali indicated he would send a team of observers, led by UN elections expert Horacio Boneo and including military expert Colonel Romeo Ferreiro. Brigadier General Tobias Dai led the government's team for military talks; Major General Herminio Morais led RENAMO's military group.[8] The government had accepted, without enthusiasm, lodging its military team in a facility of the Italian Ministry of Defense; RENAMO insisted that its delegation be lodged in a hotel. The idea of putting the military together in a sequestered site for working group sessions was then dropped. The mediators' and the observers' military experts hoped that work on military questions would begin immediately, but Raul Domingos insisted that another issue had to be resolved first.

The June 19 plenary session, at which the observers were present for the first time, adopted the agreement to amend the agenda. RENAMO, Domingos then explained, wanted to air its dissatisfaction with the way the December 1 agreement had worked and to seek improvements before moving on to negotiate a more comprehensive military arrangement. Domingos recalled he had earlier insisted that the negotiators review the work of the JVC—even though this review was not included in either the original or the revised agenda—before discussion of military questions could begin. Ambassador Incisa made a brief, factual report on the work of the JVC, pointing out that resource constraints made it difficult to monitor aggressively the entire Limpopo and Beira corridors. He recalled three other problems: the imprecise definition of the corridors, the impossibility of conducting inspections outside the corridors without first giving notice, and the argument over the government's right to use the corridors for military purposes.

The government delegation, the mediators, and the observers wanted the next plenary session to open discussion of military questions, but Domingos insisted on first obtaining an adequate response to his complaints about the work of the JVC. The mediators scheduled a plenary session on June 23, at which the two sides could state their positions on the JVC and on the item on military questions. Before this meeting, the mediators and Ambassador Incisa would consult with Guebuza and Domingos to find a solution to the problems of the JVC, and the military teams of the two parties, joined by experts from the Italian Ministry of Defense and from the observer delegations, could begin their working group sessions.

On June 23 Guebuza addressed both the issue of the JVC and the item on military questions. He said the results of the partial cease-fire signed on December 1, 1990, were positive but insufficient. He urged that the negotiations now aim at a full cease-fire, but to get to that point he would comment on alleged difficulties in the work of the JVC's military monitoring operation. Within its means the government facilitated the work of the military monitors. The government had accepted the JVC's definition of the corridors (rejected by RENAMO). For the military monitors to conduct inspections outside the corridors, where there was no cease-fire, they had to give the government advance notice of visits for their own safety. The government accepted, and RENAMO rejected, the JVC's proposal that the JVC be authorized to investigate incidents outside the corridors that violated the spirit of the December 1 agreement. The terms of the agreement limited the presence of Zimbabwean troops in the corridors and prohibited RENAMO attacks against the corridors, but they did not restrict normal use of the corridors by the government.

Guebuza then presented the government's position on military questions. There should be an apolitical army, formed from recruits from the FAM and from RENAMO. The defense forces should include an army, a small air force, and a small navy. Foreign forces should be withdrawn, and irregular armed groups disbanded. As for the security service, SNASP had already been replaced by SISE, which was organized along democratic principles. The police should be apolitical. A plan was needed to reintegrate demobilized soldiers economically and socially.

Ignoring completely Guebuza's presentation on military questions, Domingos again insisted that RENAMO's complaints about the work of the JVC's military monitoring operation be adequately answered first. He complained that the government had not given the support required by the JVC's military committee, had restricted attempts to verify the December 1 agreement, and had violated the agreement in other ways. To resolve these problems, the first step had to be to define permissible use of the corridors by the government. How could the government be trusted in conditions of a general cease-fire if it regularly violated a partial cease-fire?

The next day, Guebuza shot back, denying any government violations of the agreement. The government had given the JVC's military monitors all appropriate support within its means. The military monitors had examined RENAMO allegations and found them to be without foundation. It was time for the negotiations to move from arguments over the December 1 agreement to discussion of a general cease-fire. Domingos disagreed, insisting that until the monitoring mechanism could confirm RENAMO allegations, RENAMO could not have confidence in arrangements to supervise a general cease-fire.

Up to this point, the presence of the observer delegations had not facilitated discussion and the search for solutions. If anything, their presence stimulated Guebuza and Domingos to present and defend initial positions for benefit of their new audience.

RENAMO now released in Mozambique a "report" on the peace talks in Rome, indicating RENAMO's dissatisfaction on a number of critical points.[9] The tone of the report reflected RENAMO's isolation and fear that it might be cornered by the international community into accepting unfavorable peace terms. It accused international relief agencies, which "have the means and equipment with which to fly food and aid into many areas," of demanding that roads be opened to the interior so that FRELIMO forces could enter RENAMO areas and kill civilians. The JVC was inherently biased because "it is made up of ambassadors of the countries that have always been against RENAMO; therefore all violations carried out by FRELIMO and Zimbabwe are conveniently ignored and not denounced." Before a cease-fire, specific clauses in the constitution "that FRELIMO can apply against any party speaking in opposition to them" would have to be suspended. "If this is not done, there is a danger that opposing parties may be forced back to the bush to continue fighting in order to see these changes come about."

RENAMO's report attacked the mediators and the governments invited to send representatives to the talks. The mediators favored FRELIMO by "regarding the talks as being between a group of guerrillas and a government rather than between two political parties who have been at war for 15 years." As a consequence, FRELIMO could "play around at the negotiations when they should actually be pressured into taking the talks seriously." In a comment directed at France, Portugal, the United Kingdom, the United States, and other western countries, the report announced, "A serious difficulty is the lack of finance to assist RENAMO in negotiations." It specified RENAMO's need for a satellite telephone system, funds for travel expenses, and money to prepare for elections. "It seems the objective of the West is to finish RENAMO, not to see peace and democracy in Mozambique."

During the last week of June, while the mediators shuttled between Guebuza and Domingos to bring an end to the review of the JVC's operations, the military experts of the observer delegations and the Italian Ministry of Defense prepared a draft protocol for the item on military questions. The experts had one meeting with the government's military team, but the RENAMO military experts refused to meet until after the item had been properly introduced in a plenary session. Therefore, there was no joint working group. The mediators gradually brokered an agreement to instruct Ambassador Incisa to establish "team sites," or small operating bases for military monitoring teams, at Beira, Chimoio, and Machipanda in the Beira corridor and at Maputo, Chokwe, and Chicualacuala in the Limpopo corridor. The letter containing the agreement asked Incisa to proceed promptly. Although this letter, approved at a plenary session on July 2, resolved this issue for the purpose of the Rome talks, the team sites were never established.

RENAMO, presumably satisfied that its concerns had now been aired in front of the observers, gave a green light to discussion of the agenda item on military questions.

Humanitarian Assistance: July 1–16, 1992

While on a visit to France during late June, Dhlakama addressed the issue of expediting the delivery of humanitarian relief. "We, at RENAMO, do not ban the distribution of food aid by international organizations, but we fear that if roads are reopened the government will take advantage of that to send military reinforcements to the zones that it lost so as to get them back before the cease-fire." To avoid the criticism that RENAMO's demand that relief supplies be transported only by airplane was too expensive and impractical, he proposed "the opening of humanitarian corridors from neighboring countries, in particular from Zambia, Malawi, Tanzania, and South Africa. But the government did not allow humanitarian organizations to set up convoys from these countries."[10]

On July 2 President Chissano, who was in the United States on a private visit, met with Assistant Secretary Cohen, National Security Adviser Brent Scowcroft, and Secretary of State James Baker. Chissano and Baker discussed the peace talks, the process of political and economic reform in Mozambique, and the effects of the drought throughout southern Africa. According to press guidance issued by the State Department's Bureau of African Affairs, they "expressed concern about the slow pace of the Rome peace talks. . . in particular, delays introduced into the process by RENAMO."[11]

On July 3 Dhlakama arrived in Gaborone, Botswana, for another meeting with President Mugabe, this time hosted by Sir Ketumile Masire, president of Botswana. After preliminary contacts among aides, the main session involving Mugabe and Dhlakama took place on Saturday, July 4. In a radio interview, Dhlakama said he had proposed that Mugabe help to arrange a summit, in Botswana, between himself and President

Chissano. The two essential issues to agree on at the summit would be the formation of a small, nonpartisan army in Mozambique and suspension of antidemocratic articles in the FRELIMO constitution. Dhlakama did not propose discussing a cease-fire. Asked about the relationship between a meeting with Chissano and the talks in Rome, he explained, "It's just that in Rome everything is going to get into details. . . . What we want there is to speed things up because we do not think there will ever be positive results in Rome as long as the two leaders distrust each other."[12]

Mugabe, whose country was suffering from the effects of the drought, wanted an early cease-fire in Mozambique that would permit him to withdraw his forces from protecting the corridors without jeopardizing delivery of humanitarian relief through Mozambique to Zimbabwe as well as inside Mozambique. At the OAU summit in Dakar in late June, Mugabe and Chissano had discussed the possibility of using a summit to speed up the peace process. Following the meeting in Botswana, the next step for Mugabe was to resume contact with Chissano to see whether if there was enough shared basis in the positions of the two parties for arranging a summit.

On July 3 Domingos presented RENAMO's position on military questions at an evening plenary session. This presentation, which had been delayed for more than a month, was in substance identical with the communique issued three months earlier by RENAMO's national council. Mozambique should have a unified national army of less than 23,000 troops, made up equally of FAM and RENAMO forces, with other soldiers demobilized. Domingos rejected a request by Guebuza that the military experts of the two sides meet in a working group and insisted on hearing Guebuza's response in a plenary session scheduled for July 6.

Italy's new foreign minister, Vincenzo Scotti, was expected to meet the negotiators that evening at Sant'Egidio. While waiting for Scotti to arrive, Raffaelli invited Guebuza and Domingos to continue their discussion. Domingos raised the question of humanitarian assistance and accused the government of blocking flights into RENAMO-controlled areas. Guebuza rejected this accusation and pointed out that in any case ground access was open, except where blocked by RENAMO. Domingos, who admitted that this was a problem, then proposed that both sides agree to allow international organizations to have access for the delivery of humanitarian supplies throughout the country, including ground access as long as the roads were not then used for military purposes. Raffaelli, who was chairing the session, proposed that he invite representatives of humanitarian agencies to participate in a working group on this problem. Guebuza and Domingos accepted his proposal.

When Scotti arrived, he thanked the mediators and observers for their work. He said that the Italian government was committed to the success of the peace process, and he emphasized his confidence in Raffaelli, the Italian government's representative on the mediation team. Both Guebuza and Domingos thanked Scotti for the Italian government's support of the peace process.

As mentioned above, the impact of the drought was particularly severe in some areas controlled by RENAMO. Increased refugee flows into Zimbabwe and Zambia were one indication of how serious the situation had become in southern Mozambique. A senior U.S. government disaster relief official testified to Congress that because most famine victims are children who die when their parents migrate in search of food and water, it was necessary to prevent population movements. Mozambique, he explained, was "the most serious problem that we face from a logistical and security point of view." Relief workers would need guaranteed safe access to RENAMO-controlled areas.[13]

On July 9 the ICRC issued an emergency plan of action for Mozambique. "Never before has the situation in Mozambique been quite so explosive. . . . Vast quantities of food are needed urgently if we are to prevent thousands of people from literally starving to death."[14] Airlifting food would cost ten times more than road delivery, and in most areas there were either no runways or only earth runways on which large planes capable of delivering the quantities of food required could not land. It was an essential condition of the ICRC's relief project that both sides grant road access to areas in Gaza, Sofala, and Nampula provinces.

In two plenary meetings on Friday, July 10, the two delegations, the mediators, and the observers were joined by representatives of international humanitarian organizations, including the ICRC, the UN High Commissioner for Refugees, the World Food Program, and nongovernmental organizations (such as Caritas). Speaking for RENAMO, Domingos first asked for relief flights, but he was told that these would be in any case inadequate; he then suggested that corridors from Zimbabwe and Malawi be used to deliver food. Over the weekend, the representatives of the humanitarian organizations prepared two documents: a draft declaration of principles on humanitarian assistance and a plan for a truce.

At a plenary meeting on Monday, July 13, Domingos rejected the paper containing a truce plan, explaining that RENAMO was in Rome to achieve the conditions required for a definitive cease-fire, not a temporary truce.

On Tuesday another plenary session lasted from six in the evening until one in the morning, at which point the mediators expressed the hope that an agreement on humanitarian assistance could be signed during the next plenary session, on Wednesday evening. When that meeting began, the government objected to a provision in the draft that would allow RENAMO to send an official to Maputo to represent it on the UN-chaired committee that would coordinate and supervise humanitarian assistance operations. It took until six the following morning to resolve this point (RENAMO could appoint its representative in accordance with the procedures of the military committee of the JVC).

The July 16 Declaration on the Guiding Principles of Humanitarian Assistance announced that there would be no discrimination in delivering humanitarian assistance to afflicted Mozambicans, that there would be freedom of movement throughout the country for persons and resources traveling under the UN or ICRC flags, and that there would be freedom of movement for all persons seeking humanitarian assistance. There would be permission for air transport throughout the country as required for delivering humanitarian assistance. The parties would "permit and facilitate the use and resurfacing, where necessary, of other access roads to the affected populations," including roads from neighboring countries. The parties would negotiate to remove all obstacles to the delivery of humanitarian assistance, and they promised not to take military advantage of humanitarian assistance operations. Finally, they agreed to set up a committee in Maputo, chaired by the United Nations, to coordinate and supervise humanitarian assistance operations and stated, "Both parties undertake to comply strictly with the terms of this Declaration."

Within a week the United Nations had convened a meeting of donors in Maputo. Before the committee called for in the declaration could begin its work, RENAMO's designated representative would have to arrive in Maputo. The donors expected that a separate negotiation would still be required to open each route. If so, it would be a race against time to move adequate relief supplies to those in greatest need.

Parallel to the discussion of the humanitarian aid declaration, work had been going forward on military questions since the beginning of July. By July 7 the military experts of the observer delegations and the Italian Ministry of Defense had finished a draft protocol on military questions, based on their bilateral meetings with the government and RENAMO delegations. On July 9 the government and RENAMO military teams met together with the mediators, and there seemed to be general agreement on the structure of the new army and on a small air force and navy.

The military observers, after being briefed on the meeting, prepared an organizational outline suggesting a 24,000-troop army that included six infantry brigades, one tank brigade, and three special operations battalions.

On July 11 the mediators and two military teams met again. RENAMO now questioned the need for a separate air force and navy (perhaps because it had no trained forces to join these branches) and proposed organizing the army into forty-two small battalions of the size already used by RENAMO (200 to 300 troops). On July 15 the mediators held a meeting with both military teams plus the military observers to present a paper containing the force structure recommended by the military observers (an army of 24,000, an air force of 1,000, and a navy of 800). The FAM's Brigadier General Dai said the figures should be higher; RENAMO's Major General Morais said they should be lower. Meanwhile the military observers were conducting their own bilateral contacts with the two generals to explain the thinking behind the recommended force structure. They concluded that the government wanted a larger force to minimize the political problems of demobilizing so many soldiers and that RENAMO realized it lacked the troops to fill half the slots in a larger force.

On July 20 Guebuza and Domingos spoke to a plenary session on the preparation of the protocol on military questions. Guebuza expressed general agreement with the document being prepared; Domingos identified problems. RENAMO insisted that the name of the armed forces be changed so that its acronym would no longer be "FAM"; that the protocol require the withdrawal of all foreign forces; and that the security service, formerly SNASP but now called SISE, be disbanded. Guebuza responded that every government had some organization to collect and analyze information of strategic importance, and the Mozambican government had to have one as well. On July 21 the military delegations met again and registered their differences over force structure, the name of the armed forces, and the security service. No progress was made.

The stall in Rome was due in part to developments elsewhere. On July 19 Presidents Chissano and Mugabe met in Harare. Mugabe briefed Chissano on his meeting with Dhlakama two weeks earlier in Gaborone.[15] After meeting with Mugabe, Chissano told a press conference that he had agreed to an early summit meeting with Dhlakama and that he would do everything possible to bring about a quick cease-fire. Chissano did not announce a time or place for the summit.

On July 24 in Rome U.S. observer Hume met separately with Guebuza and Domingos. He suggested that the delegations in Rome intensify their work to prepare a set of draft principles that the two leaders could sign.

Any summit declaration should confirm the agreements already reached in the peace process, set a target date for completing the peace accord, and provide guidelines for resolving outstanding issues. Although arrangements for the summit were not yet set, both Guebuza and Domingos said that the summit should take place in Rome within a few days.

On the eve of the anticipated summit, the status of negotiations was as follows. The military experts of the Italian government and the observers, despite the small number of working group sessions or even separate discussions with the military teams from the two parties, had produced the basic draft of a protocol on military questions. Ambassador Incisa chaired these working sessions, and often the experts used the documents produced during the Angola negotiations as a point of reference. The most difficult unresolved issues were the size of the new armed forces (the observers recommended a force of 25,800 troops, which the government said was too small and RENAMO said was too large), the name for the new armed forces, and reform of the police and the security service. The military experts had prepared a basic cease-fire plan, but the parties had not yet discussed it. As for the item on guarantees, both sides agreed now on a UN role in monitoring a cease-fire, demobilization, and creation of the new armed forces, as well as in verifying the election. RENAMO made available a nine-page single-spaced memorandum identifying thirty-five provisions of Mozambique's constitution that it wanted suspended.

RENAMO gave another indication that it was preparing for a future as a political party by naming Vicente Ululu to be its first secretary-general.[16]

An African Summit in Rome: August 4–7, 1992

On Saturday, August 1, Raffaelli, Goncalves, Zuppi, and Hume discussed the outlook for the summit. Mugabe, Chissano, and Dhlakama were all set to attend; there would be preliminary meetings on August 4, and the summit would take place during the following two days. The Zimbabweans had not yet shared with the mediators any preliminary drafting they might have done on a summit declaration. The mediators thought that a declaration would have to contain three main points. First, it should reaffirm what had been done, especially on political issues. Second, to increase the sense of urgency it should set a target date for completing the negotiations and starting a cease-fire. Third, it should help resolve the tough questions regarding guarantees: guarantees on the constitution and personal security for RENAMO leaders from Chissano, logistical guarantees for RENAMO's transformation into a political party, and international guarantees for the implementation phase of the peace process. The mediators were confident that an African summit in Rome would push the process forward.

During the weekend, the mediators held four sessions with the two military teams but did not close any outstanding gaps. By Monday the Italian Foreign Ministry had made arrangements for the main events: a ceremonial opening on the morning of August 5 at Villa Madama (the Medici villa overlooking Rome); working sessions involving the Zimbabwean delegation, the mediators, and the parties; dinner on August 6; and a closing session at Villa Madama on August 7, if all went well. Mugabe, Chissano, and Dhlakama would all have individual meetings with Italy's president and prime minister.

At six on the evening of August 3, the LONRHO corporate jet touched down at Rome's airport, and Dhlakama, followed by Ululu and the rest of the RENAMO delegation, disembarked. Chissano and delegation arrived the next day at noon, and Mugabe and the Zimbabweans followed in the late afternoon. The mediators met briefly with each shortly after arrival. Mugabe told the mediators he got involved because Chissano had asked him in January to find a way to mediate between himself and Dhlakama, perhaps arranging a well-prepared summit. Chissano told the mediators he came to Rome because Mugabe had asked him to do so. None of the three told the mediators what exactly they expected would happen over the next three days.

Late in the evening of August 4 Mugabe took charge, leading the first summit session at Chissano's hotel.[17] From midnight until almost six in the morning Chissano and Dhlakama, joined only by Mugabe and Tiny Rowland, had their first meeting. That night, Chissano and Dhlakama started a necessary, if at times painful, dialogue. Chissano thought he could accommodate Dhlakama's concerns on the constitution and on personal security, but there was no agreement on the size and structure of the military.

The next morning, August 5, the meeting at Villa Madama started one hour late. The new Italian foreign minister, Emilio Colombo, opened the session, which was also attended by Botswana's foreign minister, Gaositwe Chiepe. An Italian Foreign Ministry spokesman quoted Dhlakama as having said that he came to Rome to make peace and that he trusted President Chissano. Mugabe stated that the purpose of the summit was to accelerate the peace process taking place in Rome, not to replace it. The media published pictures of the "historic handshake" between Chissano and Dhlakama.[18]

Throughout the day, a working session involving the parties, the Zimbabweans, and the mediators continued at Villa Madama. On the morning of August 6, drafting sessions on the text of a joint declaration resumed, and by midafternoon the shape of a deal was emerging. The declaration would endorse the work done so far in the Rome process. As a guarantee for RENAMO, a cease-fire would not come into force until after the assembly in Maputo had ratified the commitments made as part of the Rome peace process. The negotiators would be instructed to complete their work in Rome before October 1. When the drafting session ended in early evening, RENAMO had not yet committed itself to the text.

Before the official dinner, Mugabe and Raffaelli met with Chissano and Dhlakama to go over again the issue of constitutional guarantees. Mugabe and Raffaelli sought to reassure Dhlakama, pointing out that his political objectives were within reach. Chissano explained that he would submit the peace accord to the assembly for approval by a two-thirds majority, giving it the force of a constitutional amendment and thus precedence over previous legislation. Chissano demonstrated this procedure with concrete examples. Gradually Dhlakama came around, giving his assent to the draft declaration.

In his dinner toast President Mugabe thanked the Italian hosts and mediators. The problems in the negotiations were African problems, and the time had come to stop this war between brothers. He had become involved in the peace process to raise the discussion to the level of presidents, who could make the commitments required. The results of their talks would not then be disputed. The mediators should go forward with their work of helping the parties complete the peace agreement.

The mood at the dinner, held outside in hot, humid Roman weather, was one of expectant exhaustion. The delegations of the parties were in a good mood. Progress had been made, much work was now needed to turn this progress into detailed agreements, and the negotiators were ready to stay in Rome until a cease-fire went into effect.

The morning of August 7, the summit participants reconvened at Villa Madama for the signing ceremony. The summit declaration cited the process that led up to the summit and reconfirmed the agreements already concluded in the Rome peace process. Chissano and Domingos bound themselves to guarantee political freedom, to guarantee personal security for all Mozambican citizens, and to accept a UN role in monitoring the cease-fire and elections. The text restated the commitments from Protocol I that the government would not act contrary to the agreements reached as part of the peace process and that RENAMO, after a cease-fire, would conduct its struggle within the framework of existing state institutions. The government committed itself to submit the protocols agreed to in Rome to the national assembly for ratification. Finally, the declaration set October 1 as the target date for completing the remaining protocols foreseen in the May 28, 1991, agenda.

In his brief statement at the signing ceremony, President Mugabe called for reconciliation and cautioned the two sides not to seek military advantage in the period before October 1: "Why should one more person die from now on, when the goal of peace is finally within reach?" He described the summit as a coming together, joining African summit diplomacy to the peace process that had already been carried forward by the mediators and the Italian government.

After Sant'Egidio staff members circulated the summit declaration for signing, Chissano and Dhlakama spoke briefly, emphasizing their commitment to peace and thanking Kenyan President Daniel arap Moi for his help at the beginning of the peace process, as well as President Mugabe and the mediators. Chissano went on to thank "all those who directly or indirectly contributed toward the holding of this historic meeting, notably our friend Tiny Rowland, whose valuable work must not be forgotten; he facilitated contacts, gave advice, and helped find ways to ensure the meeting would be held."[19] Dhlakama, who was wearing a lapel button with his own picture and the message "Viva Dhlakama," expressed his commitment to peace and democracy. Like Chissano, he thanked Presidents Moi and Mugabe, as well as the mediators and the Italian government. He added, "We must not forget our private friends, notably Mr. Tiny Rowland, who worked very hard for this."[20]

After the summit, Raffaelli and Riccardi gave a radio interview. Raffaelli said that the summit had been a fundamental turning point for two reasons: The parties had agreed on a target date for concluding the entire peace accord and the head of the government and the head of the opposition had met and talked together for the first time. Riccardi said that the involvement of the international community, in addition to the mutual recognition between Chissano and Dhlakama, was reason for optimism.[21]

These remarks draw attention to the profound significance of the August summit. With the negotiations about to enter the endgame, several crucial factors had changed:

- The negotiating framework had new diplomatic credibility. Mugabe's presence at the summit gave the Rome peace process the missing element of African political legitimacy. His presence also marked a willingness to end Zimbabwe's (or earlier Rhodesia's) military involvement in Mozambique as long as the borders were peaceful and the transport corridors secure.
- The participation of the four observer governments and the United Nations, whose experts had worked to expedite negotiations by drafting technical documents for review by the parties, symbolized the probable endorsement of the results by the institutions of international diplomacy.
- By announcing the commitment to conclude a general peace accord by a specific date within this reinforced negotiating framework, the parties had done something to put pressure on themselves. They had renounced alternatives. The mediators now had much better chances of drawing them into agreement.
- The summit had reduced the fear of peace. Chissano and Dhlakama had now met, called each other brother, and exchanged promises to accept the results of peace. The international community had been present to add solemnity to this exchange of promises and to symbolize its commitment to make available means for implementation of a peace accord, especially institutional guarantees for the period from a ceasefire to elections.

At the summit, Chissano and Dhlakama had acted out the essence of the peace process: reconciliation through dialogue.

six

Endgame

The mediator's final task is to legitimize the outcome. In the Mozambique peace process the mediators had helpers who shared in this task: President Mugabe, the United Nations, and the four observer governments.

Before parties make commitments, they must be convinced that the negotiated solution, more that any available alternative, protects and promotes their interests. The process of persuasion, which helps the parties lose their fear of peace, goes forward on two fronts: explaining how the proposed solution is adequate or even favorable and demonstrating that more advantageous solutions do not exist. This persuasion starts at the beginning of the negotiation; it must be completed for commitments to be made, and then it must be maintained throughout the implementation process.

Ensuring the means for implementation makes legitimacy concrete. The parties may identify and agree on outcomes that they cannot implement without outside assistance. Or without guarantees from third parties, they may not have adequate trust to commit themselves to an agreement. The means for implementation needed to secure the outcome of the Mozambique peace process included peacekeeping, help with formation of the new armed forces, humanitarian assistance, election monitoring, and an apparatus for managing the day-to-day relations between the parties from the time of the cease-fire until elections.

A solemn, public ceremony to endorse the outcome enhances legitimacy. Such a ceremony, by boosting the status of the two parties, can be an incentive to agreement and give added weight to the commitments undertaken. It symbolizes a crucial passage in the reconciliation between the parties, the moment when by exchanging pledges they define their new relationship. The picture of the concluding ceremony at which Chissano and Dhlakama made peace showed that the UN secretary-general and leaders of foreign governments, by attending or sending their representatives, supported this outcome.

Military Questions: August 1992

On August 7, just hours after the summit had concluded in Rome, UN Secretary-General Boutros-Ghali informed Security Council members that President Chissano had told him both parties now agreed on a UN role and wanted UN assistance for the peace process. The secretary-general explained that the UN role would include monitoring a cease-fire and demobilization and verifying an election, along the lines of the UN operation in Angola.

After a break for the weekend, the military observers, UN military representative Colonel Romeo Ferreira, and Italian defense experts worked throughout August 10, 11, and 12 to prepare a cease-fire document. The document, like the initial plan given to the two delegations by U.S. military expert Snyder the previous January, described a cease-fire process that would take place in four stages: (1) In the thirty days before the start of the cease-fire, all hostile activity would cease and the UN monitoring operation would be set up. (2) In the five days after the start of the cease-fire, the forces of the two sides would be separated and begin moving toward assembly areas under UN supervision. (3) During the next twenty-five days the concentration of forces in the designated areas would be completed. (4) Demobilization would then take another five months, during which time the new unified armed forces would begin to be formed. The arrangements were based on UN experience elsewhere. The military experts planned to present this document to the government's delegation on the evening of August 12 and to RENAMO the following day.

The mediators were already aware that, despite the positive result of the summit, some problems in the draft on military questions were no nearer solution. The most difficult issue was the security service: The government said it would carry out a further reform under its own authority; RENAMO now demanded a joint command. RENAMO wanted the joint military commission that would have a role in overseeing the cease-fire and demobilization arrangements to be chaired by the United Nations; Guebuza warned that if it was not chaired by Mozambicans, national sovereignty would be infringed. Neither side had any sense of urgency about discussing the cease-fire document, despite the need for advance planning to get international monitors in place. The mediators soon realized that neither delegation was likely to request new instructions allowing it to yield on points that Chissano and Dhlakama had not discussed at the summit. The best plan for the next few weeks seemed to be to prepare mediators' texts on all remaining agenda items, discuss them with the parties, and minimize the number of issues that would have to be referred to Chissano and Dhlakama.

To prepare these draft texts the mediators, the Italian ambassador in Maputo, and the U.S. observer worked together through August 13 and 14. The draft protocol on guarantees included a calendar for the election process, drafted in light of provisions already agreed on in the protocols on the party law and on the election law and taking into account the time frames in the draft military and cease-fire protocols. Key dates in this calendar included the beginning of the election period, the investiture of the president, and the end of international supervision of the peace accord. The draft on the joint commission suggested a chairmanship rotating between the two parties, with a strong UN role in providing a secretariat. Papers on specific guarantees and constitutional questions drew together provisions from earlier protocols (for example, offices for RENAMO's activities as a political party) and the August 7 summit declaration (especially on the constitutional question). Italy offered to host the donors' conference.

The first week after the summit produced a fair amount of progress. The mediators' and observers' military group revised drafts on military and cease-fire issues and presented them to both delegations. The two delegations raised further questions, but neither seemed ready to negotiate on points left unresolved by their leaders at the summit. There were now preliminary drafts of papers on all political issues, as identified in the agenda, but these papers would not be presented to the parties until the following week. Don Matteo Zuppi intended to prepare the ground further by dining with the government delegation on Saturday and with RENAMO on Sunday.

The mediators already had a feel for what would be the hardest issues, some already on the table and others likely to arrive there:

- *Reform of SISE (formerly SNASP) and the police.* RENAMO was unlikely to implement both a cease-fire and demobilization without something being done about the police and security service that had been formed to serve a one-party state. So far the government had rejected RENAMO's proposals to abolish the security service or to set up a joint command.

- *Cease-fire timing.* RENAMO wanted full international supervision for a cease-fire, but putting international monitors in place would take a month after signing a cease-fire agreement. Would RENAMO commit itself to a cease-fire date *before* the national assembly passed legislation including guarantees, as proposed by Chissano at the August summit?
- *Sites and logistical support for the cease-fire and demobilization.* Neither side had identified sites for assembly of forces after a cease-fire or for demobilization. Considerable time was needed to arrange logistical support such as food, water, medical services, and international monitors, especially for RENAMO sites.
- *Civilian administration.* All district governors were members of FRELIMO, but RENAMO claimed effective control of much of the national territory. Would RENAMO allow the government to extend its control and administration to the entire national territory when effectively that would mean control by FRELIMO party members? Perhaps an interim arrangement for international monitoring of distribution of relief supplies along the lines of the July 16 humanitarian aid declaration would be needed.
- *RENAMO as a political party.* RENAMO had barely begun transforming itself from a rural insurgency into a political party. Dhlakama had demonstrated considerable savvy as a rebel leader, but neither he nor his colleagues had any experience at civilian administration.

The mediators already had a general plan for the time before October 1. They would need the next two weeks to go over the papers on military questions, cease-fire, and guarantees to eliminate little problems and to identify more difficult problems on which the parties would have to show greater flexibility. They could use the first two weeks in September to put creative solutions on the table and the last two weeks in September for raising the hardest issues for decision by Dhlakama and Chissano. At that time it would be easier to identify trade-offs for decision in a package deal, the type of bargaining that the strictly sequential issue-by-issue agenda had so far made impossible. The mediators suspected that reforming the security service and the police, as well as re-establishing the authority of the government's local civilian administrators, would require presidential decisions over the heads of the negotiators. The UN observer could help formulate options by indicating parameters for arrangements that the United Nations might help to implement.

At this point Ambassador Incisa returned to Maputo, where he hoped to break the impasse on implementation of the July 16 declaration on humanitarian aid. RENAMO's representative on the committee had yet to arrive in Maputo, and not one road had been opened for delivery of relief supplies.

At the beginning of the week of August 17, Zuppi feared that Guebuza and Domingos were about to widen the gap on issues of sovereignty. Guebuza repeated that the government rejected international chairmanship of the joint committee because this would violate national sovereignty; Domingos insisted RENAMO could not trust the government as chair and that the United Nations was needed to umpire the peace process. Zuppi sensed that there might be no conclusive solution for the internal aspect of the sovereignty issue because the government expected to reestablish its civilian administration throughout the country but that RENAMO did not expect to cede its local control anywhere. He wanted help in sounding out Guebuza and Domingos on these issues.

On August 17 U.S. observer Hume met with Domingos to suggest that RENAMO consider the mechanism established under the humanitarian aid declaration as a model for continuous consultations to resolve disputes over local administration. By helping this committee to play its intended role, RENAMO might establish a useful, practical precedent for resolving the civil administration quandary. Domingos took note of this suggestion, but he seemed too tired after ten weeks of nonstop negotiations to do more. He complained that the government side put forward no ideas of its own and always responded negatively to RENAMO's proposals. He suspected that the government wanted to stall rather than resolve issues early, forcing RENAMO to take or leave a package deal at the end of September. Domingos was particularly concerned about the problems of the security service and the police, especially since the government had not yet responded positively to ideas for reforming, reducing, monitoring by international means, or introducing RENAMO cadres into either force.

Guebuza likewise showed signs of fatigue. He complained that Domingos did not want a one-on-one meeting, but he admitted he had not directly asked Domingos for one. Perhaps some international role in monitoring an agreement was possible, but not in a way that would infringe on Mozambique's sovereignty. Domingos's behavior, Guebuza suggested, showed that RENAMO was willing to block humanitarian relief if government administrators helped distribute the supplies. Guebuza thought the mediators should pay more heed to the government's positions and explain to RENAMO what was possible.

On August 18 Zuppi met with the four observers and the new representative of the United Nations, Tayyeb Merchoug, to share with them the mediators' draft protocol on guarantees. Merchoug said that within two days the UN officials responsible for peacekeeping and for monitoring elections would meet to recommend parameters for an operation in Mozambique. The four observers made few comments on the mediators' text, but all suggested that the UN operation be no larger than absolutely necessary. On August 19 Secretary-General Boutros-Ghali responded to President Chissano's earlier request for UN assistance in the peace process. The secretary-general wrote that the UN role should include chairing the joint commission and providing at least 100 police monitors (two issues still in dispute between the parties). Boutros-Ghali explained that, because of the time needed to organize a peacekeeping operation properly, he wanted to send a UN survey team to Mozambique soon.

On the morning of Friday, August 22, the mediators met informally with both heads of delegation, and in the afternoon they held an informal plenary session. Domingos insisted that all outstanding issues in the protocol on military issues (the size of the new armed forces, the name of the armed forces, and reform of the security service and the police) be resolved before any discussion of the cease-fire or guarantee texts. Guebuza again rejected the idea that the joint commission be chaired by a UN representative.

Over the weekend, the mediators met separately with each delegation. Domingos provided a RENAMO redraft on military issues, confirming that the main outstanding issues were now the name and size of the new military and the reform of the security service and the police. Merchoug used his own meetings with Guebuza and Domingos to urge them to move quickly, eliminate minor problems, and concentrate on the main issues. He did not find that either delegation had a sense of urgency despite the need for advance planning for a peacekeeping operation. The government's delegation acknowledged that it might consider allowing a UN representative to chair the joint commission.

Early the next week, the mediators and observers tried to pick up the pace. On Monday morning Merchoug met with Guebuza to reinforce the points in Boutros-Ghali's letter to President Chissano. The United Nations needed permission for a UN survey team to arrive in Mozambique within the next two weeks for a ten-day visit, including access to local officials and permission to travel throughout the country. The United Nations wanted to include police monitors in a peacekeeping operation and to chair the joint commission to be set up to guide the process of implementation. Later in the day, both delegations met with the mediators for several hours to revise the draft protocol on military questions. No substantive progress was made on the difficult issues, but Guebuza acknowledged that the government would have to show some flexibility to arrive at arrangements for the police, the security service, and the chairmanship of the joint commission.

On August 26 mediators Raffaelli, Goncalves, and Zuppi met over dinner with UN representative Merchoug, Portuguese observer Antonio Sennfeldt, U.S. observer Hume, and U.S. military expert Lieutenant Colonel Jean-Michel Beraud to survey the status of the talks. Earlier in the day Raffaelli, who had recently returned from a trip to Nagorno-Karabakh as head of a Conference on Security and Cooperation in Europe (CSCE) mission, met with Guebuza for three hours on the difficult issue of the security service. The government had just put forward its own redraft of the mediators' proposal on this issue; Guebuza would not accept reform or international oversight for the security service, but the government might allow RENAMO to retain its own security service during the transition period. Merchoug had met for two hours with Domingos, telling him that no African president would cede full control over his security service, that there were no international standards for reforming such services, and that the United Nations would not take on this responsibility. RENAMO should not seek its assurances on this point from the United Nations.

Those present all predicted that the argument over the name of the new armed forces would be resolved one way or another before October 1, as would the size of the force. The government's position was unrealistic because the FAM had too many soldiers on its rolls, and even its general staff did not know their exact number. RENAMO wanted a smaller army because it had fewer troops and would find it difficult to provide enough to meet its 50 percent quota in the new army. So far there had been no discussion of parity at the various ranks, and there was no movement on the dispute over the size of the air force and navy.

This group agreed that eventually the parties would come around to practical solutions for the outstanding issues in the guarantees draft. They would probably accept a joint commission with only the parties and United Nations as members, with the UN representative as chairman. Subcommissions might involve other governments, but the number of members could be kept down. Both parties saw that South African support, particularly logistical support and mine clearing, would strengthen the process of implementation, but neither wanted to make a formal request for a South African role.

The most difficult problem, one that neither delegation seemed able to address, was how the areas with a RENAMO presence would be administered after a cease-fire. For the time being it seemed reasonable to assume that however this issue was solved in the context of the Rome talks, in fact it would have to be skillfully managed throughout the transition period by the secretary-general's representative, with some flexibility from the parties.

Going to the Top for New Instructions: September 1–12, 1992

It was now apparent that without new instructions from Chissano and Dhlakama the two delegations in Rome would be unable to resolve the key remaining issues in the protocol on military questions. Without new instructions Raul Domingos would not enter into discussions of the drafts on guarantees or on a cease-fire. Most disturbing, six weeks after the humanitarian aid declaration had been signed, its provisions remained a dead letter.

On Friday morning, August 28, the mediators and observers met at Sant'Egidio to review the situation now that the talks were almost halfway between the August summit and the October 1 target date. Zuppi briefed them on the status of the draft on military questions. The differences over the name and size of the new armed forces were gradually being reduced, and both sides were looking at ideas to resolve the argument over police reform. The biggest problem was the security service. The most the government would accept was a limited number of RENAMO representatives in the service plus some restructuring under government control. When the government rejected the mediators' redraft providing for broader reform, RENAMO, which no longer insisted on elimination and now accepted restructuring with some continuity in staff, distanced itself from the mediators' proposal as well.

The government delegation had given the mediators comments on the cease-fire paper, but RENAMO had told the mediators only that it did not have many problems with their draft. Because Domingos insisted that the protocol on military questions be completed before negotiating the next document, there had still been no discussion of the complicated arrangements for cease-fire or demobilization. The conflict over administration during the transition period was sure to make the guarantee protocol difficult to conclude. There was no progress on humanitarian issues because RENAMO refused to permit road convoys out of the coastal cities (where there were adequate supplies) and insisted on delivery only by plane or by roads entering Mozambique from neighboring countries (where supplies were inadequate).

Tayyeb Merchoug reiterated that the United Nations would not get involved in arrangements for the security service. He suggested that this issue be taken off the negotiating table in Rome for settlement elsewhere and the delegations be told to move on to other issues. For the October 1 date to be respected and for the United Nations to prepare a peacekeeping operation, the parties should be held to a strict calendar for resolving the remaining issues. Raffaelli proposed that on Saturday morning he first meet informally with Guebuza and Domingos to convey the judgment of the mediators and observers that it was necessary to take the issue of the security service off the table and move on. Unless they promised new flexibility, there would then be a plenary meeting with the parties and observers to record the decision to communicate directly with Chissano and Dhlakama on this issue. Because SISE had earlier in the week been used to control riots by an elite battalion of the FAM, no one expected Chissano to cede control over his security service.

On Saturday morning the mediators met first with the two delegations, and both agreed that a letter summing up the situation should be sent to Chissano and Dhlakama. Raffaelli was the only speaker in the full plenary session. He recalled that since the August 7 summit, talks had concentrated on military issues. Problems remaining seemed more political than technical. For the remainder of the negotiations to be completed on schedule, a decision should be reached to remove the security service from the table and to work on the guarantee and cease-fire protocols. The mediators could send letters to Chissano and Dhlakama to explain the situation and perhaps propose solutions for outstanding issues. Guebuza and Domingos assented to this procedure. After the meeting, Domingos asked whether the mediators would like to include a proposal on the size of the new armed forces in their letter.

Later that day and early evening, the mediators and observers worked on the draft of the mediators' letter and proposal on the security service. The letter described the status of the negotiations: After two months of discussions of the protocol on military questions, the delegations in Rome had to be instructed to move on to the guarantee and cease-fire documents to provide a framework for the visit of the UN survey team and conclude the negotiations by the October 1 target date. The mediators, with explicit concurrence of the observers, proposed a defense force of 24,000 troops in the army, 1,600 in the navy, and 2,000 in the air force. The mediators attached to this letter an addendum with their latest proposal on the security service. The mediators would give the letter to Guebuza and Domingos on Monday morning, and Ambassador Incisa would then deliver it to President Chissano and to Dhlakama, whom he hoped to meet in Gorongosa on Tuesday, September 1.

On September 2 the mediators held a meeting at the Italian Foreign Ministry to brief the observers. Zuppi said the mediators' letter had been given to both delegations in Rome and delivered by Incisa to Chissano. Incisa now had an appointment to give the letter to Dhlakama on Sunday, September 6, in Gorongosa. The government rejected the mediators' proposal on the security service, but it was willing to work with the mediators' suggested numbers for the size of the armed forces. Domingos, although personally ready to discuss all items on the agenda, had told the mediators he needed instructions from Dhlakama in order to do so.

The committee established by the July 16 declaration on humanitarian aid had yet to work as intended. RENAMO's representative to the committee was expected to arrive in Maputo shortly, and no roads had been opened for humanitarian shipments. RENAMO insisted on delivery by air, as in Somalia. Goncalves confirmed reports that the situation was deteriorating quickly in many places; despite adequate food supplies in the ports, starvation threatened much of the rural population. At the suggestion of UN representative Merchoug, strongly seconded by other observers, the mediators agreed to draft a letter to both sides to urge lifting of road blockades. Unless action came quickly, the situation could degenerate into widespread starvation on the scale occurring in Somalia.

The observers advised the mediators to convene the plenary session set for Friday, September 4, to put at least some pressure on the delegations to address the issues on the table. The mediators should then try to open discussion of the paper on guarantees no later than the following Monday. Boutros-Ghali, after a conversation with President Mugabe at the Non-Aligned Summit in Indonesia, dispatched a UN survey team to Mozambique.

Mugabe's interest in getting a settlement in Mozambique was increasing. Because of the drought, large numbers of Mozambicans were threatened with starvation; because of the war, relief supplies could not be delivered. Unless this situation could be turned around, many rural Mozambicans were expected to move toward the food supplies in the transport corridors and then onward toward the border with Zimbabwe. RENAMO's representative on the humanitarian assistance committee finally arrived in Maputo on September 2, but he had yet to attend a meeting of the committee. No roads had been opened.

An argument between Guebuza and Domingos consumed the one-hour plenary session on September 4. Guebuza insisted that the mission of the new defense forces be to protect the "independence, sovereignty, and territorial integrity" of the country; Domingos did not want independence mentioned first. The two made no effort to discuss substantive issues such as numbers for the defense force, the police, or the security service. At the end of the meeting, the mediators signed letters to Chissano and Dhlakama urging that the impasse on delivery of humanitarian assistance be overcome immediately. The next plenary session was set for Tuesday, September 8, two days after Ambassador Incisa was expected to meet with Dhlakama at Gorongosa to deliver the mediators' letter of August 31 and to discuss how the negotiations might be completed by the October 1 target date.

When Incisa's airplane landed in Gorongosa, it sank deep into the sandy air strip. He was obliged to spend the night at RENAMO's headquarters before a second plane could come to fix the first and take him out. Dhlakama told Incisa that before discussions on the guarantees and cease-fire protocols could begin, all items in the draft on military issues, except for the security service, had to be settled. He accepted the mediators' figure of 27,600 for the defense forces. Regarding the police, he rejected the joint monitoring commission proposed by the mediators and asked for RENAMO to enter a joint command. He demanded that the security service be abolished, but RENAMO might be willing to compromise. Once the service had been purged of its criminal elements, two RENAMO deputy directors could be appointed to flank its FRELIMO director; alternatively, a new service limited to gathering national security information could be created during the transition period.[1]

Dhlakama said humanitarian aid could be delivered only in the sequence given in the July 16 declaration: by air, by land from other countries, and then by road from the ports. He saw that eventually this issue would be tied into the problem of civilian administration. He wanted RENAMO to retain control in its areas in the period before elections, providing administration in part through the traditional authority relations that FRELIMO had worked to supplant. If food was to be distributed in these areas, this benefit should be associated with administration by RENAMO, not by FRELIMO.

In his report to Rome, Incisa commented on the positions of the two presidents. Both intended to maintain full control over the negotiations and had kept their delegations under strict instructions since the August summit. Both seemed personally committed to a successful conclusion of the negotiations by the October 1 target date. The mediators' proposals on military questions were a good basis for resolving those issues. But the two leaders were still poles apart on the security service.[2]

On September 8 the mediators briefed the observers on Incisa's meeting with Dhlakama. The plenary meeting that followed the briefing accomplished nothing. The mediators then held bilateral discussions with the two delegations over the next two days. The mediators saw that the negotiating situation was changing in two ways: Progress on arrangements for implementation would have to involve discussions with the United Nations, and RENAMO was getting more concerned about its future and looking more toward finding a way to have an effective share of power during the transition period. The mediators insisted it was essential to maintain the basic balance agreed to by the parties eleven months earlier in Protocol I: RENAMO would accept the administrative legitimacy of the state, and the government would accept a significant measure of international supervision. Looking at the impasse in negotiations, Goncalves asked the question that was on the minds of the observers: Did either of the parties sense any urgency or responsibility because mass starvation threatened?

U.S. observer Hume met separately with each delegation to encourage them to show more flexibility with the mediators. He emphasized to the government's negotiators that every effort should be made to reach an agreement by the October 1 target date and that the urgency of the drought permitted no delay. The survey visit then being conducted by the United Nations could help this process if it resulted in a practical discussion of arrangements for UN involvement in a cease-fire, in managing the transition period, and in conducting elections.

In his next meeting Hume reminded Domingos of the fundamental understanding in Protocol I that RENAMO would obtain elections with international supervision in exchange for observing a cease-fire and accepting the government's legitimacy as administering authority. Domingos retorted that there could be no legitimate government until elections. Turning immediately to some of the tough issues on the table, he asked why the government would not accept RENAMO cadres in the police if it had accepted RENAMO troops in the defense force. He questioned why the government could not agree on numbers for the defense force by accepting a solution close to the mediators' proposal. He reviewed RENAMO's fears about the security service and insisted that something had to be done to control this force in the period before elections. Recalling that before the August summit the two sides had resolved a number of issues in informal working sessions, Domingos said that contacts were now more difficult. He had met only twice with Guebuza one on one, both times at his own initiative in August 1990. Now he worried that Guebuza might try to manipulate such a meeting to push back the October 1 target date.

Hume suggested that RENAMO could solve many of its concerns by cooperating with the UN survey mission to Mozambique. The United Nations had just sent civilian and military survey teams to consider the needs for monitoring civilian administration and peacekeeping during the period between a cease-fire and elections. For UN experts the question of legitimacy related to preservation of essential state functions, not constitutional theory. RENAMO should work with the United Nations on the police question, picking up on the idea of international police monitors. RENAMO should facilitate the team's travel throughout Mozambique, not just to Gorongosa, so that it could plan for a peacekeeping operation. Now that RENAMO's demand for a significant UN role was becoming a reality, RENAMO would have to adjust to the new situation and learn to play by UN rules.

During the week, meetings in Maputo marked the changing relationship between the parties and the international community. The two UN survey teams met with representatives of both parties and began to prepare reports on what a UN role in implementing the peace agreement would involve. The donor members of the committee for humanitarian assistance prepared and presented a plan for food deliveries that included some deliveries by air and some by roads originating in other countries, but most by roads spreading out from the ports and transport corridors. The government accepted the plan, but RENAMO rejected it, insisting on deliveries only by air or by practically impassable roads along the border. The committee prepared a message to the parties: "Air delivery to all the needy population is not possible, and can only be a short term, last resort measure. Land delivery by truck convoys, flying ICRC or UN flags, to the locations presented must begin immediately to save the vulnerable populations." Although RENAMO offered the committee a counter-proposal, there would be no agreement on delivery of relief supplies before a cease-fire.

On the evening of September 11, Domingos introduced a new proposal to give RENAMO members positions at all levels of the police force, establish a joint command, and make the police subordinate to the joint military commission. In the series of sharp exchanges that followed, Guebuza objected to the idea of a joint command. He rejected this proposal, in effect a demand for power sharing in the transition period, as a violation of the entire basis of the negotiation, as stated in Protocol I. Domingos simply observed that no agreement had yet been reached on the protocol on military questions, so RENAMO's proposal was timely. To end this exchange, Zuppi stated that while the mediators would examine RENAMO's text, the mediators' last draft would stay on table for discussion.

At the end of the meeting Guebuza announced that the government accepted the proposals in the mediators' letter of August 30. It was ready to discuss all remaining items on the agenda, and it approved delivery of relief supplies by any means to any location in Mozambique.

After the meeting, the observers met with the mediators to analyze the situation. Only two full working weeks remained before October 1. So far the two delegations had not worked sensibly on military questions; it seemed that the main work of preparing specific arrangements for guarantees and the cease-fire would in fact be based on the reports of the UN survey teams. Despite the mediators' letter, Dhlakama had not given Domingos the authority to discuss all remaining items, and none of the observers thought the two delegations in Rome could settle the remaining issues. To meet the October 1 target date, the format for the negotiations would have to change: Chissano and Dhlakama would have to be involved in preparing solutions at least on the police, on the security service, and on RENAMO's desire for power sharing in the civilian administration.

Portuguese observer Sennfeldt suggested that, working from the drafts for the protocols on guarantees and cease-fire already prepared by the mediators and observers and from the comments the two delegations had made, the mediators and observers should revise these texts. The Italian government, in collaboration with President Mugabe, could send a message to the parties to come to Rome several days early for the October 1 summit; the letter should explain that draft documents had been prepared but a few items required further discussion before the summit. This proposal, which offered one way to structure the closing phase of the negotiations, stimulated interest.

Summit Preview: September 13–15, 1992

The United Nations now had two survey teams in Mozambique. The first, led by Horacio Boneo, concentrated on arrangements for elections. Because the protocols on the political party and the election laws had already been signed, his group had a concrete framework for its talks with local officials, which included two meetings with President Chissano and two separate meetings with Foreign Minister Mocumbi. Discussions regarding the implementation phase of the peace process would have to take place with UN officials, operating under instructions from headquarters in New York. The Security Council would have to be kept informed of significant decisions. The informality of the peace process, symbolized by the low-profile mediation team, was ending.

The second survey team, led by Noel Francis, examined the requirements for peacekeeping. The situation they found was grim: an estimated 3 million displaced persons inside the country and 1.5 million refugees in neighboring countries; inadequate information on the location of minefields put down by both sides, the possibility that soldiers facing demobilization might drift into banditry, and such danger for travel on roads outside the Limpopo and Beira corridors that armed military escorts were required. The team's work was hampered because the two sides had not yet negotiated the details of the cease-fire document; in particular, there was no list of assembly points at which the troops of the two sides would congregate. The size and difficulty of a peacekeeping operation would be directly affected by the number and location of these points, as well as by the availability of such basic infrastructure as potable water, electric power, housing, and transport.

This second team met with President Chissano and with President Dhlakama, and it traveled to a number of sites outside Maputo. Its work drew attention to an issue that the negotiations in Rome avoided. If international forces were to take over the role played by foreign troops in providing security for the three transport corridors (including the Nacala corridor still protected by Malawian troops), the number of peacekeepers would be at least several thousand, and they would be responsible for providing security, not just for monitoring. This new task, if taken on, would overturn the Rome experts' assumption that the peacekeeping operation might require only several hundred lightly armed observers.

When President Mugabe went to Brussels to attend a Sant'Egidio-sponsored prayer for peace on Sunday, September 13, he met twice with the mediators to discuss the impasse in negotiations. They reported that the delegations in Rome were unable to resolve the problems of the size of the military, the reform of the police and the security service, and the arrangements for civilian administration in RENAMO areas. If Chissano and Dhlakama could be induced to deal with these issues directly, perhaps the two delegations in Rome could negotiate the draft protocols on guarantees and a cease-fire in the time remaining before October 1.

After his encounter with the mediators, Mugabe decided to arrange another Chissano-Dhlakama meeting to generate a breakthrough on these issues. He secured Chissano's agreement to meet again with Dhlakama, and he made sure that President Masire would welcome the two leaders in Botswana. Once again Tiny Rowland was induced to play a key role in getting Dhlakama to participate; Rowland would fly Dhlakama from Nairobi to Gaborone on his corporate jet. Mugabe, having made the necessary arrangements, could stay home.

The next day, September 14, Dhlakama responded to Assistant Secretary Cohen's letter urging that the peace accord be completed by October 1. After rehearsing RENAMO's concerns on a number of points, including the security service, he explained RENAMO's position on civil administration:

> RENAMO controls a large part of Mozambican territory and has its own civilian administration. Therefore RENAMO and FRELIMO must reach an understanding on those areas. This means RENAMO will administer its own areas until a new government is installed after democratic elections, therefore ensuring peace in the cease-fire period before elections. This does not mean Mozambique would have two administrations or two internationally recognized governments; we only want to avoid putting out of work our people now doing the administration and replacing them by FRELIMO members, a senseless step. For such a thing to happen would be the undoing of RENAMO.[3]

Neither Guebuza nor Domingos showed any flexibility in their positions during three plenary sessions the following week. Progress was insignificant. The mediators worked out with the observers a plan to prepare final mediators' texts on the four remaining protocols (military questions, guarantees, cease-fire, and donors' conference) for discussing the issues with the two delegations, to present the texts to Chissano and Dhlakama a few days before the actual summit, and then to work out solutions directly with the leaders. During one meeting with Domingos, UN observer Merchoug insisted that the United Nations could not implement an agreement that provided for the government and RENAMO to administer the country in parallel—but Domingos simply countered that RENAMO must retain administrative control over its own areas.

On Friday, September 18, Deputy Assistant Secretary Davidow again stopped in Rome on his way to Angola. He supported the idea that Chissano and Dhlakama should meet before the concluding summit to resolve the main outstanding issues. Both Guebuza and Domingos admitted that their leaders would have to resolve these issues directly. While

Davidow was meeting with the two delegations, Chissano and Dhlakama were already en route to Gaborone for the encounter engineered by Mugabe.

Chissano and Dhlakama met for several hours the evening of September 18 and again the following morning, when they emerged to announce that they had reached an agreement on the outstanding issues. They planned to sign the final documents by October 1 at a summit meeting in Africa. As explained to the press in Gaborone and shortly thereafter by Guebuza and Domingos to a plenary session in Rome, the leaders had agreed that the number of troops in the new Mozambican national defense forces would be 30,000. They modified the mediators' proposal to establish an oversight commission to monitor the security services, making it a national commission with all members Mozambicans. They would set up a similar body to monitor the reform and activities of the police. According to Guebuza, they "more or less agreed" on the difficult question of civilian administration in the RENAMO areas, with RENAMO civilian cadres being left in place but government administrators allowed to establish a presence throughout the country.

The Gaborone mini-summit produced a breakthrough on the political level, but it produced no texts on these difficult issues. The work of drafting was again left to the mediators, supplemented by discussions by Ambassador Incisa with Chissano and with Dhlakama.

On September 22 President Chissano addressed a special session of the Assembly of the Republic. He emphasized the contributions to the peace process made by Presidents Moi, Mugabe, and Masire and by Tiny Rowland, and he said the final overall peace agreement would be signed in Africa on October 1. He explained that in Gaborone he had agreed to oversight commissions for the police and security services as a confidence-building gesture toward RENAMO.

The negotiators in Rome did what they could to prepare for the concluding summit. The mediators produced clean copies of their texts on guarantees, cease-fire, and the donors' conference. They wrote to Chissano and Dhlakama recalling the numerous actions, such as appointing members of various commissions, that both sides had committed themselves to perform in the first month following a cease-fire; it seemed neither side had given thought to the concrete requirements for implementing the agreements they were about to sign. Chissano and Dhlakama indicated on September 24 that the summit would in fact be held in Rome.

With just one week remaining before the concluding summit, the situation was strange. Domingos admitted that he was without instructions and thus effectively unemployed. There were no agreed texts on the tough issues of the police, the security service, and the extension of the state's civilian administration into RENAMO areas. Worse, the negotiating teams had not seriously discussed the draft protocols on guarantees and cease-fire, which would be the key documents for guiding the implementation of the peace process. There was little understanding of the many actions that would be required to transform the declaration of peace by both leaders into a stable, internationally monitored cease-fire. The only positive signs were that Guebuza and Domingos called each other "my brother" for the first time at a plenary session on September 25, and that the two delegations began to fraternize more easily before and after meetings.

Summit Finale: September 28 to October 4, 1992

The concluding summit in Rome was the ultimate act of legitimization for the mediation process based at Sant'Egidio.

On September 28 Dhlakama sent a letter to the mediators identifying several "very delicate" matters that should be resolved before the summit: arrangements for assembling the two parties' troops under international supervision after a cease-fire and for administration of RENAMO-controlled areas. As he had written in his letter to Assistant Secretary Cohen two weeks earlier, he insisted that RENAMO's civilian infrastructure stay in place until after the installation of a democratically elected government. Dhlakama mentioned the need for the government and the international community to provide relief supplies and economic support to these areas. He sent along new RENAMO proposals on the security service, the police, and the civilian administration that departed somewhat from the concepts that he and Chissano had discussed at Gaborone.

The mediators issued their response in a press release the next day: "The mediators and observers hope that RENAMO's leader will reconsider and come to Rome, in order to permit the solution of all issues needing clarification through direct meetings with President Chissano, guaranteeing the conclusion of the negotiations."

President Chissano arrived in Rome with a large delegation on September 29. Presidents Masire and Mugabe were soon bound for Rome. Tiny Rowland meanwhile waited in Nairobi for Dhlakama, but RENAMO's leader was delayed in Gorongosa. When Dhlakama arrived in Nairobi, he insisted on meeting with President Moi before flying on to Rome. He arrived for the summit at six in the evening of October 1.

The main issues were still unresolved. During the afternoon, the negotiators had met at Sant'Egidio, but neither side offered new positions on the eve of the summit. The most positive sign was that the RENAMO delegation arrived in new Italian suits—a good indication that they were making final preparations for a signing ceremony. The Italian Foreign Ministry made arrangements to host the ceremony on October 2 or 3.

UN Secretary-General Boutros-Ghali was already in communication with the president of the Security Council regarding arrangements to implement a peace accord. In a letter dated September 29 he described the joint commissions being established and explained that "past experience has shown that such joint machinery functions best when the chairmanship is entrusted to an impartial third party." He pointed out the need for early precision in the number and location of sites where the forces of the two sides would be asked to assemble. He cited the provision calling for the withdrawal of all foreign forces and said that UN peacekeepers might be needed to provide security for the vital Nacala, Beira, and Limpopo transport corridors. In any case, "it would not be possible for the United Nations to establish more than a token presence in Mozambique within 30 days" of a peace agreement, with full-scale monitoring of a cease-fire possible only after that date. In concluding his letter, Boutros-Ghali cited the risks of humanitarian disaster unless there was full cooperation from RENAMO and the government for the international community's efforts to deliver relief supplies. To reinforce these points with the parties he sent Under Secretary-General James Jonah to the summit.

While President Chissano wanted to meet Dhlakama to finalize the text on the remaining issues, Dhlakama insisted that the two leaders meet only after an agreement had been reached through the mediators. To avoid pressure to make concessions, he put off meeting the other leaders, such as Presidents Mugabe and Masire, South African foreign minister Pik Botha, and Portuguese secretary of state for cooperation Jose Durao Barroso, who had come to Rome to push the parties toward agreement and to attend the signing ceremony.

Raffaelli, joined by Riccardi, Goncalves, and Zuppi, shuttled between Dhlakama's headquarters at the Forum Hotel and Chissano's, either in his own suite at the Grand Hotel or nearby in Mugabe's suite at the Majestic. The negotiations at this level concerned only the security services, the police, and civilian administration. President Chissano insisted that the commissions set up to supervise these elements of national administration not have international membership and not be subordinate to the joint commission to be chaired by the United Nations. Dhlakama wanted maximum RENAMO participation on these commissions. Throughout the day and the early morning, the mediators went back and forth between the two sides.

Discussion of the arrangements for a cease-fire was left to heads of delegation working at Sant'Egidio. Although they managed to simplify the text prepared by the mediators' and observers' military experts, no concrete decisions were reached on the most important provision: the location of assembly points for the troops of both sides. To the observers it seemed simply that neither delegation was adequately prepared to address specifics. The best the two delegations could do was to state a maximum number of such points, with agreement to identify exact locations to the United Nations later.

Assistant Secretary Cohen arrived early Saturday, October 3, to join the other dignitaries for the signing ceremony. First he met at Sant'Egidio with the mediators, who were exhausted from another long night of shuttling between Chissano and Dhlakama. Riccardi explained that there was now agreement on the cease-fire protocol, on the police, and on the security service. To oversee the reform and activities of the police and the security services, separate commissions would be created whose members would be Mozambican citizens appointed by the president, some on the nomination of RENAMO. The commission on the security service would provide reports to the joint commission chaired by the United Nations only on request; the commission on police would report to the joint commission regularly. But civilian administration—or rather arrangements to reassure Dhlakama that RENAMO's infrastructure would not be displaced—still had to be worked out.

Throughout the day, the mediators continued their work. The other dignitaries watched from the sidelines. Only Tiny Rowland, who was telling Dhlakama to conclude the deal, seemed able to get through to RENAMO's leader. Particularly for Durao Barroso and Cohen, the election results from Angola were a major cause for concern; Savimbi had lost the election, but there was no sign he would accept that result. At the end of Mozambique's peace process, as at its independence, developments in Angola could have an impact on Mozambique. As the mediators moved back and forth between the hotels where Chissano and Dhlakama were holding court, it seemed the final stage of negotiations was designed as public proof that each leader had insisted on the best possible deal for his own side.

Shortly before midnight President Chissano said he would like to meet in his suite at the Grand Hotel with Assistant Secretary Cohen. Chissano explained in detail to Cohen how the text on civilian administration had been modified throughout the day (Protocol V, section III, point 9). The resulting text was complicated and confusing. RENAMO accepted that public administration must conform to the laws in force. Only citizens resident in RENAMO-controlled areas could be employed by administrative institutions there. The government would not disturb traditional authorities that actually exercise administrative authority. And a national commission to be formed by the parties would "facilitate collaboration and good understanding" between the Ministry of State Administration and the administration in the RENAMO-controlled areas. During Chissano's long explanation, Zuppi called to say Dhlakama had just confirmed his acceptance of this text. The signing ceremony was set for the next morning.

On leaving Chissano's hotel, Cohen gave a brief interview to a Portuguese radio journalist to appeal to Savimbi to accept the results of the UN-supervised election in Angola.

After these three days of intensive negotiations, the signing ceremony took place late Sunday morning, October 4. The setting, the formal treaty room of the Italian foreign ministry, gave maximum solemnity to the occasion, and the presence of many high officials reinforced that impression.

President Mugabe spoke before the documents were signed: "This event we are going to witness now—the signing of a cease-fire and general peace agreement—is an event that will forever remain memorable in the minds and hearts of the people of Africa, especially those of Mozambique. It is an event which marks a transformation of relations amongst them, from relations of conflict to relations of peace, from war to peace." He told the parties that, after the pains of war, "today is not the day of judgment. It is the day of reconciliation. Today is not the day when we should examine who was right and who was wrong. Today is the day when we must say we are all right. Both are right in being party to the process of peace. We cannot escape that process."[4] Mugabe acknowledged that Zimbabwe had permanent interests in relations with its neighbor Mozambique. Once Zimbabwe had participated in Mozambique's war, but now it wanted to be a partner in Mozambique's peace.

Archbishop Goncalves, who had suffered under the conflict from the beginning and constantly worked and prayed for its end, spoke with obvious emotion. Because he was the human link between the war and the mediation, Goncalves had played perhaps the most pivotal role in the peace process. As a Mozambican and man of God, he was overjoyed to witness this moment of reconciliation. "I want to sing and dance with the Mozambican people during this period of peace, joy, and reconciliation."[5]

Guebuza and Domingos then signed the protocols on military questions, on guarantees, on a cease-fire, and on a donors conference. Chissano and Dhlakama signed the overall peace accord.

The two leaders spoke briefly. Chissano thanked individually many of the officials at the ceremony who had supported the peace process; he expressed hope for the future but spoke little about the actual agreement.[6] Dhlakama gave the same message of peace and hope, and he pledged that for RENAMO victory was obtaining a democratic system for all Mozambicans, not winning an election. "There is no hatred, and as of now our relations will be dominated by the rule of trust," Dhlakama said. "The armed struggle will be replaced by a political and democratic one. The people will choose those whom they feel are the best from among us and other political forces."[7]

At the end of the ceremony, the mediators handed over the signed texts to UN Under Secretary-General James Jonah to carry back to New York for presentation to the secretary-general.

The mediators had done a splendid job of securing legitimacy for the overall peace agreement. Presidents Chissano and Dhlakama said they were convinced and committed. The international community, represented most immediately by the United Nations, was willing to help with implementation. A ceremony of full pomp and circumstance solemnized the agreement. Still, the agreement itself was flawed.

The most sensitive elements for implementing this agreement were contained in the protocols on military questions, guarantees, and the cease-fire. These documents would govern the processes of demobilizing 70,000 of the estimated 100,000 troops of the two sides and creating a new national armed forces, of reforming the police and the security service, and of reestablishing civilian administration throughout the country. Despite the efforts of the mediators and the observers, especially their military experts, the parties never seriously discussed the practical elements of these documents. They had little idea how to set up, let alone operate, the complex set of commissions, committees, and subcommittees they insisted on creating to manage these arrangements. They had stipulated a timetable that they could not possibly keep to, even in the first weeks after a cease-fire. Worse, in fifteen years of civil war, neither side had shown the organizational capacity to overcome these defects.

Despite the optimism of the ceremony, the outlook was guarded.

The role of the United Nations would now be pivotal. Unlike the mediation team, the UN secretary-general could deal with the parties from a strong institutional basis, which included standard operating procedures for peacekeeping, management of humanitarian relief programs, a network of relations with states providing funds or personnel, and the requirement of Security Council authorization. Because of the defects in the agreements, the process of implementation would have to be constantly preceded or accompanied by a process of renegotiation.

Reconciliation was the goal when the parties met at the Community of Sant'Egidio twenty-seven months earlier. Judged by that goal, enormous progress had been made, with the parties committed to a relationship of dialogue, not war. The documents signed on October 4 were a milestone for the peace process and a map for the ongoing journey of reconciliation. The parties, helped along by the United Nations, could now start another stage of that journey.

Epilogue

Two questions remain. What next for Mozambique? What lessons does the Mozambique peace process offer for resolving conflicts in the 1990s and beyond?

What Next?

On October 9, 1992, Secretary-General Boutros-Ghali informed the Security Council of the main features of the peace agreement,[1] and in resolution 782 (1992) the Security Council welcomed the agreement and authorized the secretary-general to appoint a special representative, to send a team of military observers, and to report on what was needed to set up the UN operation called for by the agreement. The secretary-general appointed Aldo Ajello to be his special representative.

The peace agreement came into force on October 15, after publication of the legal instruments adopted by the Assembly of the Republic. However, the parties were not in direct contact, and none of the joint mechanisms called for by the agreement were in place. On November 4 the special representative appointed the Supervisory and Monitoring Commission, which then set up its subcommissions to deal with the cease-fire, with demobilization, and with forming the new armed forces.

On December 3 Boutros-Ghali proposed to the Security Council a mandate for ONOMUZ, the UN operation in Mozambique. This mandate, based on the Rome protocols, included four elements:

- *Political*—to facilitate implementation by chairing the commission.
- *Military*—to monitor the cease-fire, demobilization, and withdrawal of foreign forces and "to provide security . . . in support of the peace process, especially in the corridors."

- *Electoral*—to assist and monitor the electoral process.
- *Humanitarian*—to coordinate and monitor humanitarian assistance operations.[2]

In addition the secretary-general instructed his special representative to reopen with the parties the issue of including police monitors as part of ONOMUZ.

In recommending to the Security Council that it approve the establishment of ONOMUZ, the secretary-general observed, "But however great the resources the United Nations decides to devote to Mozambique, the general peace agreement will not be implemented unless the Mozambican parties make a determined effort in good faith to honour their commitments. The efforts of the United Nations can only be in support of theirs."[3] On December 16 Security Council resolution 797 (1992) authorized the establishment of ONOMUZ.

Soon Special Representative Ajello was renegotiating with the parties as well as directing ONOMUZ. Dhlakama announced on January 7, 1993, that he would not go ahead with assembly of forces and demobilization until most UN forces were deployed;[4] in addition RENAMO demanded that 65 percent of ONOMUZ troops be deployed in RENAMO-controlled areas.[5] The government hampered deployments by drawing out negotiations over a status of forces agreement with ONOMUZ until May 14, 1993. Despite the commitments made on October 4, the two sides failed to agree with ONOMUZ on assembly points, which were needed to begin demobilization; the calendar for the cease-fire and demobilization slipped. Because RENAMO's delegation in Maputo faced logistical problems, the joint commission to oversee formation of the new armed forces was not in operation nine months after the October 4 agreement. These accumulated delays, caused primarily by the parties, compelled Special Representative Ajello to renegotiate the time frames in the agreement, postponing the date for elections from October 1993 to October 1994. The parties seemed incapable of setting up the complicated set of mechanisms called for in their agreements.

In his April 2, 1993, report to the Security Council, Boutros-Ghali observed, "It is essential to have the necessary conditions to allow RENAMO to assume its proper role in the political and social life of Mozambique. This is a serious problem which has to be resolved by the Mozambicans as soon as possible, if the peace process is to succeed." In fact the closely related issue of civil administration, negotiated so tortuously during the final days of the Rome peace process, remained a source of tension. As long as all provincial governors and senior administrators were FRELIMO party members, RENAMO instinctively wanted its own piece of the action in the civil administration to compensate for the programmed loss of its military forces. The Rome text on civil administration had papered over the problem with a complicated procedural mechanism, not solved it.

In contrast, the situation on the ground was better than could have been expected. Despite a few minor incidents, both sides respected the cease-fire. Zimbabwe withdrew its troops from the Beira corridor in April 1993, and Malawi withdrew its forces from Nacala in June. By the end of June, ONOMUZ had deployed its total strength of 6,100 military personnel. The humanitarian crisis was eased when the drought and the war both ended, and humanitarian agencies could redirect operations to help with resettlement of refugees, displaced persons, and demobilized soldiers.

By June 1993, despite real progress in setting up the UN operation, the secretary-general had to call on both parties to accelerate the implementation of the peace process. The people of Mozambique desired the return of peace, but the agreement had to be implemented. "This promising environment will remain fragile and the future of the country will continue to be uncertain, at best," said Boutros-Ghali. "The United Nations will of course continue to sustain and assist in the implementation of the peace process, but it cannot move it forward by itself. Much would now depend on the two Mozambican parties themselves; their intentions will be increasingly judged by their deeds."[6]

Over the next year the secretary-general, Special Representative Ajello, ambassadors in Maputo, and the parties monitored, adjusted, and renegotiated the arrangements for implementation. A trip by Boutros-Ghali helped unblock the process for demobilization and establish the election commission. Later modifications were made to reduce the role of the UN military component and to expand the work of police monitors; extra help was solicited for forming the new national army; and creative paths were found to obtain the funds needed for RENAMO's change into a civilian political party. Finally, agreement was reached to schedule elections for late October 1994.

The secretary-general could prod the parties because the dynamics of third party involvement changed during the period of implementation. Unlike Sant'Egidio, the United Nations controlled an armed force of more than 6,000 soldiers, coordinated relief supplies equal to half Mozambique's gross national product, operated from a defined institutional structure, and benefited from the explicit authorization of the Security

Council. Given the devastation of Mozambique, the tragedy of its history, and the failure of its leaders to work together, a strong UN role could help reconciliation move forward.

What Lessons Does the Mozambique Peace Process Offer?

***First,** the peace process should center attention on the core of the conflict.*

Although this conflict had international and regional connections, it was fundamentally a domestic conflict fought by Mozambicans. National identity was not at issue: Both sides at least agreed on being Mozambicans. The argument was over who should govern and how.

This domestic conflict had to be separated from other conflicts. The end of the Cold War removed any connection that Mozambique had to superpower rivalry, and by the late 1980s the most significant international involvement in Mozambique was the delivery of massive amounts of humanitarian aid. The international factors affecting the conflict became favorable to a settlement.

Given the trend toward detente among the states in southern Africa, the regional factors affecting the conflict might be reduced. In 1990 the mediators were wise to opt for a first agreement that gradually removed Zimbabwean forces from the conflict between Mozambicans. This agreement, even if implemented imperfectly on the ground, opened a basis for dialogue between RENAMO and the government of Zimbabwe. President Mugabe, once FRELIMO's comrade in arms, eventually became the senior statesman supporting the peace process.

Throughout the peace process, the mediators emphasized that their goal was reconciliation among Mozambicans. Peace could not be built on the basis of a victory of one party over the other. Because there was no argument over national identity, the purpose of the negotiations was to help the parties live together in one community. It would be inadequate to help the two parties accommodate themselves to living side by side in separate communities, as might be appropriate in other conflicts. Gradually the conflict changed from who should have power to how the government should be chosen and how it should govern. This change took time.

In concentrating on the conflict among Mozambicans the mediators developed a profound understanding of how to resolve this conflict, and they applied this understanding faithfully.

***Second**, the peace process should take place within a framework designed and built to order.*

By 1990 the parties had already released a number of conciliatory messages through third parties, including Mozambican church leaders. Perhaps a third party could encourage and facilitate these attempts at dialogue. The major powers made no real attempt to organize a peace process, and a series of efforts by states in the region stalled. The Community of Sant'Egidio, which for a decade had worked to reduce the suffering that this conflict had inflicted on ordinary Mozambicans, had access to and credibility with both sides. Unlike a state, it could facilitate a dialogue without the status of the two parties becoming the threshold issue. With the blessing of the church and the backing of the Italian government, it organized the first meeting between the parties.

What role should this third party (actually four individuals with different backgrounds and institutional connections) play? Mozambicans answered this question. RENAMO insisted on a mediator, but the government preferred direct talks. When the parties could not agree on which African state might be asked to mediate, they asked the four observers already facilitating the talks to act as mediators.

The choice was fortunate. These individuals, having no leverage to apply, relied on the skills and qualities of any good mediators: competence, a positive relationship with both parties, creativity, patience, and determination. They persuaded the parties simply by encouraging dialogue, reducing their fears, and making reconciliation seem possible. Of course the parties could force awkward choices on such mediators, but in any negotiation the parties have the final word on how they negotiate and on what terms they settle.

The next piece of the framework put in place was the agreement regulating the status of the parties. The government would retain its legitimacy and administrative authority, as conditioned by an eventual peace agreement; RENAMO would have specified rights as a political party after a cease-fire; and during the period between a cease-fire and elections the United Nations would be asked to monitor the implementation of the peace process. This formula did not conclusively settle the issue of status, as seen in the debate over administrative arrangements in RENAMO-controlled areas, but at least both sides recognized guidelines for dialogue and compromise.

Eventually, when negotiations turned from political to military questions, the framework was expanded to include other states and the United

Nations as observers. The new participants were expected to reinforce the dialogue by providing expert advice on military questions, by lending their credibility to agreements reached, and by making outside resources available for implementation. Their role was to support a process already under way, even when this meant making the best of the flawed arrangements demanded by the parties. To have insisted on removing those flaws during the negotiations rather than accepting solutions and seeking adjustments during implementation might have postponed or derailed the emerging peace agreement.

The concluding element in the negotiating framework was the series of meetings with African leaders, especially President Mugabe. These meetings reduced RENAMO's fear of peace and gave African legitimacy to the negotiating process. States that had once been involved in the conflict among Mozambicans now wanted to foster reconciliation.

As negotiations neared their end, arrangements were made to maintain the dialogue in the future. During implementation the parties would have to work together with the UN special representative. By October 4, 1992, the process of reconciliation was well under way, and it was reasonable to hope that the cease-fire would hold, that the contending armies would be demobilized and a new national defense force be formed, and that elections would be held.

Third*, the character of the peace process should be gradually transformed to accelerate changes in relations between the parties.*

How did this happen over time? After fifteen years the two parties suffered from a stalemate that was the equivalent of an impending military defeat. Government units were ill disciplined and mutinous, and RENAMO had trouble resupplying itself from an already devastated countryside. The drought made the hurting worse. Both sides wanted to find an alternative to stalemate and destruction.

The mediators helped the parties find that alternative. Because this conflict was essentially domestic, the solution had to be found in a new relationship between the parties. The mediators concentrated on developing mutual recognition and respect, rather than relying on outside leverage to push the parties together. Their first step was to begin a dialogue between the parties that could open the way to reconciliation. Eventually the parties could agree on their own solutions.

Other governments—including both African states (Botswana, Kenya, Malawi, South Africa, and Zimbabwe) and donors (France, Italy, Portugal, the United Kingdom, and the United States)—supported this process.

The two governments active throughout, albeit in different roles, were Italy and the United States. During the negotiations, these governments put friendly pressure on Chissano and Dhlakama to stay engaged in dialogue and to commit themselves to specific solutions. Their growing involvement helped to persuade the parties that the risks of peace were less than the dangers of war.

African statesmen helped the mediators with the problem of closure. The May 28 agenda established what the negotiations would include but not when they would conclude. President Mugabe played a key role in arranging the August summit that produced a commitment to complete the negotiations by October 1—a commitment that finally generated a sense of urgency.

***Finally**, the process of dialogue and reconciliation must continue beyond the signing of the peace agreement.*

Because both neighbor and donor governments had interests in a settlement, they could be counted on to carry forward their involvement in the peace process from Rome, where negotiations were the main concern, to Mozambique, where implementation would be the challenge. They would insist on continued dialogue between the parties as the way to solve problems with implementation. When the final agreement was signed in Rome on October 4, everyone understood that the next stage was for the parties to return home to build their new relationship inside Mozambique.

Although the parties did not adhere to the timetable specified in the Rome agreements, the process stayed on track. Special Representative Ajello activated the dialogue between the government and RENAMO to address problems; ambassadors of key regional and donor governments urged that the parties overcome obstacles to implementation; and both the secretary-general and the Security Council explained that the international community would supply resources only for progress, not deadlock. Because the dialogue for discussing problems and adjusting commitments stayed alive, the process could move forward.

During the first meeting at Sant'Egidio in July 1991 Andrea Riccardi quoted Pope John XXIII: "Let us seek more that which unites than that which divides." Despite occasional setbacks, frequent confusion, and the mediators' lack of diplomatic standing, they kept to this method of work. They helped the people of Mozambique to find a road ahead that is better than their immediate past. Now the government and RENAMO, assisted by the United Nations, must travel that road.

Notes

1. Seeds of Conflict

1. William Finnegan, *A Complicated War: The Harrowing of Mozambique*, University of California Press, Berkeley, 1992, p. 27.

2. Finnegan, *A Complicated War,* p. 29.

3. Chester A. Crocker, *High Noon in Southern Africa: Making Peace in a Rough Neighborhood*, W. W. Norton and Company, New York, 1992, pp. 43–50.

4. Finnegan, *A Complicated War*, pp. 108–11.

5. *New York Times*, February 9, 1975, p. IV, 3:3.

6. *New York Times*, May 12, 1975, p. A, 4:5.

7. Finnegan, *A Complicated War,* p. 112.

8. Crocker, *High Noon in Southern Africa*, p. 217n.

9. *New York Times*, October 1, 1983, p. I, 3:4.

10. Finnegan, *A Complicated War*, p. 119.

11. *New York Times*, March 3, 1984, p. I, 7:1.

12. Roberto Morozzo della Rocca, "Fratelli nemici," unpublished manuscript, Rome, 1993, p. 10.

13. *Country Reports on Human Rights Practices for 1985*, U.S. Department of State, p. 226.

14. Crocker, *High Noon in Southern Africa*, p. 248.

15. George P. Shultz, *Turmoil and Triumph: My Years as Secretary of State*, Scribner's, New York, 1993, p. 1117.

16. See Allen Isaacman, "Mozambique and Regional Conflict in Southern Africa," *Current History,* vol. 86, no. 520, May 1987, pp. 213–16.

17. Finnegan, *A Complicated War*, p. 65.

18. *Mozambique New Times*, no. 3, May–August 1992, p. 8.

19. Crocker, *High Noon in Southern Africa,* p. 245.

20. *Country Reports on Human Rights Practices for 1985*, p. 223.

21. Finnegan, *A Complicated War*, p. 250.

22. For another view of RENAMO, see Michael Hughes, "Marxism under Siege: RENAMO Tightens the Vise in Mozambique," *Soldier of Fortune*, March 1987, p. 46.

23. Community of Sant'Egidio, *War Never Again: Religioni e Pace*, Morcelliana, Rome, 1990.

24. Roberto Morozzo della Rocca, "Sant'Egidio: La via romana alla pace," *Limes*, no. 3, 1993, pp. 69–82.

25. Finnegan, *A Complicated War*, p. 58.

26. Merle L. Bowen, "Economic Crisis in Mozambique," *Current History,* May 1990, p. 217.

27. Chester A. Crocker, "U.S. Policy Toward Mozambique," *Current Policy*, no. 983, U.S. Department of State, Bureau of Public Affairs, Washington, 1987.

28. *Country Reports on Human Rights Practices for 1989*, p. 237.

29. *New York Times*, August 1, 1989, p. I, 3:1.

30. *Activita della Santa Sede 1988*, Vatican Press, p. 803.

2. Starting a Dialogue

1. *Mozambique New Times*, no. 3, May–August 1992, p. 9.

2. *New York Times*, February 11, 1989, p. I, 14:1.

3. *Il Messagero*, April 21, 1989.

4. *New York Times*, July 18, 1989, p. A, 8:1.

5. *New York Times*, August 1, 1989, p. I, 3:1.

6. *New York Times*, August 1, 1989, p. I, 3:1.

7. *Washington Post,* October 23, 1989.

8. *Noticias*, August 16, 1989.

9. Finnegan, *A Complicated War,* p. 311.

10. *New York Times*, March 14, 1990, p. A, 15:1.

11. *New York Times*, June 13, 1990, p. A, 4:3.

12. Finnegan, *A Complicated War*, pp. 311–12.

13. *New York Times*, June 14, 1990, p. A, 7:1.

14. Morozzo della Rocca, "Fratelli nemici," p. 32.

15. *Radiogiornale*, Radio Vaticano, July 12, 1990.

16. Morozzo della Rocca, "Fratelli nemici," p. 44.

17. *New York Times*, August 15, 1990, p. A, 5:1.

18. *Osservatore Romano*, September 20, 1990, p. 1.

19. Morozzo della Rocca, "Fratelli nemici," p. 54.

20. *New York Times*, November 13, 1990, p. A, 10:3.

3. Ordering the Peace Process

1. Morozzo della Rocca, "Fratelli nemici," p. 64.

2. Morozzo della Rocca, "Fratelli nemici," p. 83.

3. Morozzo della Rocca, "Fratelli nemici," p. 73.
4. Morozzo della Rocca, "Fratelli nemici," p. 77.
5. *Le Monde*, August 12, 1991, p. 6.
6. *Mozambique New Times*, no. 3, May–August 1992, p. 7.

4. Helping Negotiations Along

1. Andrea Bartoli speaking at a conference on regional conflicts hosted by the United States Institute of Peace in Washington, D.C., July 1992.
2. Joint press statement, Geneva, November 2, 1991.
3. Morozzo della Rocca, "Fratelli nemici," p. 89.
4. *Mozambique New Times*, no. 3, May–August 1992, p. 7.
5. Afonso Dhlakama, news conference, Gorongosa, December 21, 1991, Voice of RENAMO.
6. Dhlakama, news conference.
7. FBIS MB0308102892, Radio Mozambique, August 2, 1992.
8. *Mozambique New Times*, no. 3, May–August 1992, p. 7.
9. FBIS MB0102173492, Voice of RENAMO, January 30, 1992.
10. FBIS MB1202094292, Voice of RENAMO, February 12, 1992.
11. FBIS MB1802114592, Voice of RENAMO, February 18, 1992.
12. Morozzo della Rocca, "Fratelli nemici," p. 98.

5. Expanding the Framework

1. FBIS MB1104091992, Voice of RENAMO, April 11, 1992.
2. FBIS MB1104091992.
3. Morozzo della Rocca, "Fratelli nemici," p. 100.
4. FBIS MB1704060692, Voice of RENAMO, April 12, 1992.
5. Dhlakama-Cohen joint press statement, Lilongwe, Malawi, April 25, 1992.
6. Communique of the presidential cabinet, Gorongosa, June 6, 1992, point 12.
7. Agreed minute, June 19, 1992.
8. For an article describing General Morais, see Hughes, "Marxism under Siege."
9. "Report from the Cabinet and President of RENAMO concerning the Present Situation of Mozambique and Current Peace Talks in Rome," dated July 1992 (released before June 26, 1992), referred to by Luis Serapiao at United States Institute of Peace conference, Washington, D.C., July 1992.
10. FBIS LD0107013692, Radio France International, June 28, 1992.
11. Department of State, AF Press Guidance, July 2, 1992.
12. Voice of America interview with Dhlakama, July 8, 1992.
13. Andrew Natsio, assistant administrator of the Bureau for Food and Humanitarian Assistance, U.S. Agency for International Development, testimony before House of Representatives subcommittee, June 9, 1992.

14. "Emergency Plan of Action: Mozambique, Proposed by the ICRC for July to December 1992," issued by the ICRC, Geneva, July 9, 1992.

15. FBIS MB0308102992, Radio Mozambique, August 2, 1992.

16. FBIS MB0108102192, Radio Mozambique, August 1, 1992.

17. *New York Times*, August 6, 1992, p. A, 3:1.

18. *The Economist*, August 15, 1992, p. 33.

19. FBIS MB0708134792, Radio Mozambique, August 7, 1992.

20. FBIS MB0708134792, Radio Mozambique, August 7, 1992.

21. Radio Vaticano, August 11, 1992.

6. Endgame

1. *Il Giornale*, September 7, 1992, p. 3.

2. Morozzo della Rocca, "Fratelli nemici," p. 117.

3. Morozzo della Rocca, "Fratelli nemici," p. 120 (translation by Hume from Italian).

4. FBIS MB0410200392, Radio Mozambique, October 4, 1992.

5. FBIS MB0410185392, Radio Mozambique, October 4, 1992.

6. FBIS MB0410155692, Radio Mozambique, October 4, 1992.

7. FBIS MB0410133192, Radio Mozambique, October 4, 1992.

Epilogue

1. UN documents S/24642 of October 9, 1992, and S/24635 of October 8, 1992 (text of general peace agreement).

2. S/24892, December 3, 1992, p. 5.

3. S/24892, December 3, 1992, p. 15.

4. S/25518, April 2, 1993, p. 2.

5. S/26034, June 30, 1993, p. 2.

6. S/26034, June 30, 1993, p. 7.

Bibliography

Books

Activita della Santa Sede 1988, Vatican Press.

Community of Sant'Egidio, *War Never Again: Religioni e Pace*, Morcelliana, Rome, 1990.

Country Reports on Human Rights Practices for 1985 and *Country Reports on Human Rights Practices for 1989*, U.S. Department of State, Washington, D.C.

Crocker, Chester A., *High Noon in Southern Africa: Making Peace in a Rough Neighborhood*, W. W. Norton and Company, New York, 1992.

Finnegan, William, *A Complicated War: The Harrowing of Mozambique,* University of California Press, Berkeley, 1992.

Morozzo della Rocca, Roberto, "Fratelli nemici," unpublished manuscript, Rome, 1993.

Shultz, George P., *Turmoil and Triumph: My Years as Secretary of State,* Scribner's, New York, 1993.

Vines, Alex, *RENAMO: Terrorism in Mozambique*, Indiana University Press, Bloomington, 1991.

Articles

Bowen, Merle L., "Economic Crisis in Mozambique," *Current History*, vol. 89, no. 547, May 1990, p. 217.

Crocker, Chester A., "U.S. Policy Toward Mozambique," *Current Policy,* no. 983, U.S. Department of State, Bureau of Public Affairs, Washington, 1987.

Hughes, Michael, "Marxism under Siege: RENAMO Tightens the Vise in Mozambique," *Soldier of Fortune*, March 1987, p. 46.

Hume, Cameron R., "The Mozambique Peace Process," *The Diplomatic Record 1992–93,* Westview Press, Boulder, Colorado, 1994.

Isaacman, Allen, "Mozambique and Regional Conflict in Southern Africa," *Current History*, vol. 86, no. 520, May 1987, pp. 213–16.

Morozzo della Rocca, Roberto, "Sant'Egidio: La via romana alla pace," *Limes*, no. 3, 1993, pp. 69–82.

——, "Mozambique: Out of the Ruins of War," *Africa Recovery Briefing Paper No. 8*, UN Department of Public Information, May 1993.

Documents

UN document S/24635, issued on October 8, 1992, contains the texts of the general peace agreement signed on October 4, the seven protocols signed during the course of the negotiations, the joint communique of July 10, 1990, the agreement of December 1, 1990, the declaration on humanitarian assistance signed on July 16, 1992, and the joint declaration signed in Rome on August 7, 1992.

Index

African neighboring states proposed as mediators, 30–31, 35, 49
Agenda
- agreements, 43, 49, 71
- amendment, 102, 103
- political system items, 62
- redrafted, 63

Ajello, Aldo, 141–43, 147
Almirante, Joao, 32
Andreotti, Giulio, 18, 20, 32, 35, 36, 38, 46–47, 57, 79
- peace process support, 18, 20, 32
- Round Two, 35, 36, 38

Angola
- election, 136, 137
- impact of independence movement on Mozambique, 6–7

Angola Peace Accords as model, 64, 66, 75–76, 88, 96, 111, 118
Arbitration definition, 26

Babb, Glenn, 66
Banda, Hastings Kamuzu, 84
Bartoli, Andrea, 73
Beira port
- importance to Zimbabwe, 7

Beira transport corridor, 5, 7, 9
- security issues, 103, 131
- team sites, 106
- Zimbabwean troops, 43, 44, 56, 57, 143

Beraud, Lt. Col. Jean-Michel, 123
Berlin Conference of 1885, 4–5
Berlinguer, Enrico, 17–18, 46
Bilateral discussions, 67, 91, 92, 95, 102, 105, 135
Boneo, Horacio, 103, 130
Botha, P. W., 11, 22
Botha, Roelof "Pik"
- at peace accords ceremony, 3
- suggestion that U.S. act as mediator, 27

Botswana
- host for Mugabe-Dhlakama talks, 106–7
- representative at summit, 112

Bottai, Bruno, 96
Boutros-Ghali, Boutros, 103, 118, 122, 126, 135, 141–43
Britain
- development of transport in Mozambique, 5
- as observer at peace talks, 101

Bush, President George, 31
Byerly, John, 81, 84

Cabora Bassa Dam repair agreement, 22
Caritas relief efforts, 101, 108
Carrington, Lord Peter, 10
Casaroli, Cardinal Agostino, 31
Castro, Jose, 99
Cease-fire
- agenda position, 52, 61
- Christmas truce, 47, 80, 81–82
- early talks, 14, 27, 34, 42, 46
- four-phases proposal, 84, 118, 120
- FRELIMO's draft proposal, 64
- importance to humanitarian relief efforts, 98–99

Cease-fire *(cont.)*
  localized, 55, 58, 103
  monitoring issues, 97, 98, 100, 104, 111, 143
  temporary truce proposal, 100, 108
Celli, Mgsr. Claudio, 58, 79
Ceremony purpose in peace process, 117–18, 134, 137–39
Chiaromonte, Sen. Gerardo, 17
Chiepe, Gaositwe, 112
Chimoio airport, 47, 54, 55, 56–57
China
  support for FRELIMO government, 8
Chissano, Joaquim
  agreement on political parties, 56
  election as president, 13
  first steps toward reconciliation, 21–22, 41
  offer to establish a multi-party system, 35–36
  at peace accords ceremony, 3, 138–39
  political concessions, 58–59
  talks with Dhlakama, 112–14, 133
  talks with mediators, 69, 99, 110
  Washington visits, 13, 31, 106
Church leaders' role in peace process, 27, 30–31, 58, 145
Civil administration, 142–43
  FRELIMO government's position, 136–37
  RENAMO's position, 132
Civilian casualties
  due to forced relocations, 10
  due to starvation, 10
  in RENAMO attacks, 15
Cohen, Herman J.
  acceptance of request for help in ending the war, 28, 35
  meetings with Chissano, 99, 106
  meetings with Dhlakama, 44, 100
  meetings with Domingos, 40, 62
  meetings with mediators, 63, 65–66, 136
  statement commending Round One talks, 36
Cold War tension's impact, 4, 6, 23
Colombo, Emilio
  at peace talks, 3, 112
Colonial era, 4–6
Communist government. *See* FRELIMO
Community of Sant'Egidio. *See* Sant'Egidio
Constitution issues
  FRELIMO government's guarantees, 113
  mediators' proposals, 81, 89–91, 102, 107
  RENAMO's concerns, 57–59, 63, 82–83, 87, 98, 111
Control commission. *See* JVC
Coutinho, Admiral Rosa, 6
Creagan, James, 36
Crocker, Chester A., 20, 21, 22
Cuba
  military aid to Angola, 7
  military aid to Mozambique, 9

Dai, Tobias, 66, 103, 110
Davidow, Jeffrey, 57, 65, 66, 69, 75, 87
  Geneva meetings, 101
  meetings with Chissano, 87
  meetings with Dhlakama, 57
  meetings with mediators, 65, 66, 69, 75, 87
  Rome meetings, 96, 132–33
de Klerk, F. W., 22, 28
de Michelis, Gianni, 32, 79, 90
Demobilization, 111, 118, 143
Dhlakama, Afonso
  demand for secure communications with Rome, 40, 42, 55–56, 58, 60, 61, 105
  early peace signals, 23
  in Geneva, 75
  in Lisbon, 60, 76
  meetings with U.S. officials, 44, 89–90
  Nairobi talks, 28
  at peace accords ceremony, 3, 138–39
  RENAMO leadership, 13–14
  in Rome, 57, 58, 79, 92
  Round Two agenda, 36, 41
  self-imposed isolation in Gorongosa, 65, 66, 68–69, 70
  talks with Chissano, 112–14, 133
  talks with Incisa, 101, 127–28
  talks with Mugabe, 106
"The Dhlakama Papers," 59
Displaced persons, 44, 97, 131, 143. *See also* Refugees
Domingos, Raul
  Lisbon visit, 35
  meeting with Guebuza, 36–37
  meeting with ICRC, 39
  Nairobi visit, 35

Domingos, Raul *(cont.)*
at peace accords ceremony, 138
proposal on political party law, 76–77
RENAMO military leadership, 13
RENAMO negotiator at peace talks, 32, 33, 34, 38, 42, 47, 122, 124, 125, 128
RENAMO official contact with U. S., 76
Round Two negotiations, 36
Round Six talks broken off, 67
Round Ten negotiations, 103, 104
Donor nations, 20, 97–99, 109
Donors' conference, 119
dos Santos, Cardinal Alexander, 27, 32
Drought, 12, 69, 91, 92, 96, 97–100, 107, 108
Durao Barroso, Jose
at Lisbon conference, 65, 76
at peace accords ceremony, 3
in Rome, 90

Economic crisis, 12, 19–20, 97–98
Elections issues
Angola accords proposed as model, 66
draft protocol, 119
mediators' role, 74, 80–91
mediators' single text, 86–87
opposing positions, 82–85
options for organizing, 42
"side-by-side" text, 86
UN role, 130
European population in Mozambique
colonial era, 5
post-colonial era, 5

Facilitation definition, 25
FAM
Cuban military advisers, 9, 19
offensives, 40–66
RENAMO's insistence that name be changed, 110
Soviet military supplies, 19
strength of forces, 19, 123
unsuccessful efforts, 11, 125
Fein, Bruce, 59, 64
Ferreira, Col. Romeo, 103, 118
FNLA, 6–7
France
official observer status, 101, 102
Francis, Noel, 131
FRELIMO
foreign supporters, 8
founding, 8
FRELIMO government. See also FAM
amnesty program for insurgents, 21, 58
constitution, 57, 58, 113
economic policy, 10, 13, 20
Marxist-Leninist policies, 11, 57, 58
perspective in initial peace moves, 28, 30
political system, 62
religious persecution, 12, 17, 27
shift toward West, 12, 20–21, 23, 58
twelve-point plan, 27, 28
Frente da Libertacao de Mocambique. *See* FRELIMO
Friedman, Townsend B., Jr., 69, 75, 76, 77
Fugit, Edward, 28

Gaborone mini-summit, 133
Geneva talks, 42, 69, 75
Gersony, Robert, 15
Gersony report, 15, 36, 88
Goncalves, Don Jaime
initial peace moves, 27, 32
meetings in Africa, 41
at peace accords ceremony, 3, 138
role in peace process, 17–18, 33, 46, 126, 128
Good offices definition, 25
Gorongosa headquarters of RENAMO, 13, 20, 40, 42, 43
airstrip, 66, 127
demand for secure communication line with Rome, 40, 55–56, 58, 61, 105
FRELIMO threats, 68
Government legitimacy issue, 64, 66, 67, 77
Guebuza, Armando Emilio
cease-fire discussion, 42, 104
FRELIMO government negotiation, 32, 33, 37–38, 122–23, 125
meeting with Domingos, 36–37
as minister of the interior, 13
at peace accords ceremony, 138
Gwenjere, Matteus, 8

Hama Thai, Antonio, 66, 80
Holy See diplomacy, 31

Humanitarian efforts, 74, 91–93, 143
  air routes for delivery of food, 107, 108, 127
  Declaration of Guiding Principles, 109
  discussions, 106–11, 127
  donor nations, 20, 97–99, 109
  ground routes for delivery of food, 44, 98, 99, 100, 102, 106–9, 126–27
  ICRC's role, 60, 96
  international committee proposed, 101
  RENAMO's concern, 106
  Rome negotiations, 42, 60, 96
  Sant'Egidio's role, 18
  security issues, 100
  urgency, 52, 67, 69, 92, 96–98, 100, 101, 108, 111, 128
Humanitarian organizations, 108. *See also* ICRC
Hume, Cameron
  named U.S. observer, 56, 76
  talks with Dhlakama, 57, 92
  talks with Domingos, 78, 110, 121, 128–29
  talks with Guebuza, 78, 90, 110
  talks with mediators, 56, 75, 78, 111, 123, 128
Hunguana, Teodato, 10, 30, 32

ICRC, 42, 44, 55, 60, 74, 91, 101
  proposals for humanitarian relief, 39, 40, 96–97, 108
Implementation, 117, 141–43
Incisa di Camerana, Manfredo
  as chairman of JVC, 47, 53, 54, 68, 99, 101, 103
  draft of summit declaration, 101, 111
  talks with Dhlakama, 101, 127–28
  "team sites," 106
Independence movement, 5–6, 8
  leadership, 8
Initial peace moves
  agreement to meet at Sant'Egidio in Rome, 30–32
  basic agreements, 49
  church leaders' role, 27, 30–31
  FRELIMO government's perspective, 28, 30
  meetings in Africa, 26–30
  RENAMO's perspective, 28–30
International assistance in peace talks, 68–70, 80, 88, 91, 93, 96, 144
International Committee of the Red Cross. *See* ICRC
International involvement in peace talks
  observers, 101–3, 115, 138–39
Italy. *See also* Sant'Egidio
  support for peace process, 18, 74, 88, 93, 96, 108, 119, 147

Jackson, William, 81, 84
John Paul II, Pope, 16, 18, 21
Joint Verification Commission. *See* JVC
Jonah, James
  at peace accords ceremony, 3, 135, 138
Jose, Gen. Pascoal, 54, 56, 58
JVC, 44–45, 47, 56
  as monitor of cease-fire, 82, 104
  reports, 53–55, 103

Kaunda, Kenneth, 28
Kenya. *See also* Nairobi talks
  RENAMO's dependence on for travel documents, 35, 74
  RENAMO's insistence on Kenya as mediator, 34–38, 40
Khrushchev, Nikita S., 5
Kiplagat, Bethuel, 26, 32, 39–40, 42, 69

Lecocq, Randall, 36
Limpopo corridor
  security issues, 57, 103, 131
  team sites, 106
  Zimbabwean troops, 19, 44, 53
Lisbon conferences, 35, 60, 65, 76
LONRHO corporation, 29, 32, 112

Machel, Samora
  leadership of FRELIMO, 8
  meeting with pope, 18
  presidency, 9, 11–13
  Washington visit, 12, 18
Machipanda attack, 58
Malawi
  importance of transport corridors, 97
  military aid to Mozambique government, 19, 29
  military security for Nacala corridor, 19, 29, 131, 143
  Nacala corridor agreement, 48, 55
  peace talks, 32, 60, 63, 69, 80, 84
Marxist-Leninist government, 11, 57, 58

Masire, Sir Ketumile
host for Chissano-Dhlakama talks, 132
host for Mugabe-Dhlakama talks, 106–7
at peace accords ceremony, 3
Matsangaissa, Andre, 13
Mazula, Aguiar, 31, 32, 40
Mediation definition, 26
Mediation diplomacy, 26, 51–52, 73, 95, 117, 144
Merchoug, Tayyeb, 122–23, 125–26, 132
Military issues, 95, 96, 100, 101, 104
draft protocol, 105–6, 109–11, 118–26
RENAMO's position statement, 107
Military Verification Committee, 47
Missionaries and mission schools, 13, 18, 54
MNR, 10
Mobutu Sese Seko, 6
Mocumbi, Pascoal M., 28, 31, 99, 131
Moi, Daniel arap
support for peace talks, 26–27, 28, 69, 114
Mondlane, Eduardo, 8
Morais, Maj. Gen. Herminio, 103, 110
Movimento Popular da Libertacao de Angola. *See* MPLA
Mozambican Armed Forces. *See* FAM
Mozambican National Resistance. *See* MNR
MPLA, 6–7
Mucache, Jeremias, 27
Mugabe, Robert G.
Davidow visit, 89
early peace talks support, 28
at peace accords ceremony, 3, 138
presidency of Zimbabwe, 10
summit meeting support, 98, 107, 110, 114–15, 131–32, 144, 146, 147
ZANU refuge in Mozambique, 7
Murrial, Agostinho, 32

Nacala corridor to Malawi
importance in the north, 5, 19
moratorium on RENAMO attacks, 29, 55
protection by Malawian troops, 19, 29, 131, 143
Nairobi talks, 28, 29, 30, 35, 39, 69
Ndau tribal group, 4, 13
Neighboring states' interests in Mozambique's peace, 5, 7, 9, 19, 84
Neto, Agostinho, 6
Nkavandame, Lazaro, 8
Nkomati Accord, 11, 12, 14
Noticias articles on the peace talks, 31

OAU, 83, 107
"On Fundamental Principles," 67
ONOMUZ, 141–43
Operation Production, 10, 13, 20
Organization of African Unity. *See* OAU

Pagliara, Giocondo, 18
Peace accords ceremony. *See* Summit meetings
Perito, Robert, 42
Podgorny, Nikolai, 9
Political issues, 47, 48, 55, 70–71, 74. *See also* Constitution issues; Elections issues
Portugal
in Mozambique's colonial era, 4–6
as observer at peace talks, 76–77, 90, 101, 102
Prayer for peace day, 16, 131
Press statements, 31, 56, 64, 70, 76, 79, 83, 87, 100, 102, 110, 112
Pretoria cease-fire talks, 14
Protocol I, 67, 70, 98, 113, 128
Protocol II, 79–80
Protocol III, 92
Protocol V, 136–37

Radio broadcasts on the peace talks, 35, 64, 106, 114, 137
Voice of America, 57
Voice of RENAMO, 91, 98, 99
Raffaelli, Mario
meetings in Africa, 41
at peace accords ceremony, 3
peace process efforts, 123, 125
Round Two private meetings, 40
Round Five discussions, 59–60
as spokesman for Sant'Egidio peace talks, 35, 37, 38
Reagan, President Ronald, 12, 13, 21
Reconciliation, 26
Refugees, 39, 44, 60, 97, 108, 131, 143. *See also* Displaced persons
Religious repression by FRELIMO government, 12, 17, 27

RENAMO
- commitment to peace process, 3, 23, 28, 30, 75, 81
- constitution concerns, 57–59, 63, 82–83, 87, 98, 111
- demand for secure communications link with Rome talks, 40, 55–56, 58, 61, 105
- demands regarding ONOMUZ, 142
- draft constitution, 59
- foreign contacts, 11, 14
- foreign support, 11, 12, 14, 20
- headquarters, 13, 20
- human rights violations, 11, 14–15
- leadership, 13
- loss of members to amnesty program, 21, 58
- military forces, 14, 20
- political party law proposal, 77
- position statements, 61, 63, 105
- recruitment for insurgency effort, 10–11
- sixteen-point position paper, 28–29
- transformation to political party, 56, 57, 59, 81, 88, 92–93, 111, 120

Resistencia Nacional Mocambicana. See RENAMO

Rhodesia. *See also* Zimbabwe
- impact of independence struggle on Mozambique, 4–5, 7, 9–10
- military targets in Mozambique, 7, 9–10
- ZANU sanctuaries in Mozambique, 7, 9–10

Riccardi, Andrea
- leadership of Sant'Egidio, 15
- as mediator, 17–18, 32–33, 147
- Nairobi meeting, 39
- offer of Sant'Egidio's support, 28
- at peace accords ceremony, 3
- report on Round One, 35

Roberto, Holden, 6

Rome peace talks. *See also* Summit meetings
- agreements, 70, 79–80, 92
- final agreement, 137
- first meeting between Chissano and Dhlakama, 112–14
- host. *See* Community of Sant'Egidio
- international assistance, 68–70, 80, 88, 91, 93, 96, 144
- international observers, 101–3, 115, 138–39
- observers/mediators named, 33
- target date for conclusion, 99–100, 111, 114

Round One
- agenda discussions, 34
- cease-fire discussion, 34
- FRELIMO government delegation members, 32
- official observers, 33
- opening statements, 33
- options for mediation, 34
- RENAMO delegation members, 32

Round Two
- foreign troops issue, 38
- FRELIMO government's positions, 37, 40
- Kenya-as-mediator issue, 35, 36, 37
- mediation options, 39, 40, 41
- observers-as-mediators agreement, 41
- RENAMO's position, 36–37
- U.S. position, 36, 40

Round Three
- agenda agreed upon, 43
- cease-fire discussions, 42
- humanitarian relief issue, 42
- options for organizing elections, 42
- transport corridors issue, 43–45
- U.S. support, 41–42

Round Four
- transport corridor security, 52–59
- Zimbabwean troops, 52

Round Five
- political issues, 59–64

Round Six
- government legitimacy, 64, 66, 67
- political issues, 66, 68
- Protocol I draft, 67
- talks broken off, 67

Round Seven
- Protocol I draft considered, 68–70
- Protocol I draft signed, 70

Round Eight
- political party issues, 74–80
- political party law proposal by RENAMO, 77

Round Nine
- constitution issues, 87–91
- election law discussion, 80–91
- military discussions, 91
- Protocol III signed, 92

Round Ten
cease-fire document, 108–9
constitution issues, 102
humanitarian relief discussions, 106–9
international observers, 102–3
Rowland, Roland "Tiny," 29, 32, 74, 84, 112, 114, 132, 136

SADF, 7
Sant'Egidio, Community of
founding principles and vocation, 15–17
as host of peace talks, 3, 33, 145
leaders, 15–16
prayer for peace day, 16, 131
Savimbi, Jonas, 6, 136, 137
Scotti, Vincenzo, 107–8
Security issues
humanitarian efforts, 100
transport corridors, 41, 44–45, 53, 57–58, 93, 103
unrest in neighboring states, 9
Security service discussions, 12, 61–63, 104, 110, 111, 118, 119–20, 123–26
Sengulane, Bishop Dinis, 27
Sennfeldt, Antonio, 123, 130
Shangana tribal group, 4, 13
Shona ethnic group, 7, 13
Shultz, George, 12, 20
Silvestrini, Archbishop Achille, 18
SISE, 104, 110, 119, 125
SNASP, 12, 61, 62, 104, 110
Snyder, Lt. Col. Charles, 42, 81, 84, 118
Soares Veloso, Gen. Jacinto, 11
Sodano, Archbishop Angelo, 30, 31
Sommaruga, Cornelio, 42
South Africa
armed involvement in Mozambique, 4
cease-fire talks, 14
Nkomati Accord, 11, 12
RENAMO support, 11, 12, 14, 20
security strategy, 6, 11
support for peace process, 66, 89, 123
South African Defense Forces. *See* SADF
Soviet Union
support for FRELIMO government, 9, 19, 70
Starvation of masses threatened, 10, 91, 93, 100, 108, 126, 128
State security service. *See* SISE; SNASP
Summit meetings, 134–38
African leaders in attendance, 111–14
agreement to set time and place, 110–11
draft documents, 101, 110–11
essential issues, 107
"historic handshake," 112
peace accords ceremony, 3, 114, 134–39
proposals, 84, 96, 98–99, 106–7
signing ceremony, 113–14

Tanzania
military aid to Mozambique government, 19
Tauran, Msgr. Jean-Louis Tauran, 31
Tete corridor, 19, 55, 60
Thatcher, Margaret, 10, 21
Third-party involvement, diplomatic doctrine on, 25–26
Thomashausen, Prof. Andre, 59, 64
Transport corridors. *See also* Beira transport corridor; Limpopo corridor; Nacala corridor to Malawi
definition discussions, 48, 54, 104
foreign security for, 19, 29, 44, 53, 143
importance to neighboring states, 5, 7, 9, 19
RENAMO attacks, 14–15
security discussions, 41, 44–45, 53, 57–58, 93, 103
Treaty of Tordesillas, 4
Tribal groups, 4. *See also* Ndau; Shangana

Ululu, Vicente
as member of RENAMO's negotiating team, 32
proposal on political party law, 76–77
RENAMO responsibilities, 13–14
as RENAMO's first secretary-general, 111
UN High Commissioner for Refugees, 108
Uniao Nacional para a Independencia Total de Angola. *See* UNITA
UNITA, 6, 66
United Kingdom. *See* Britain
United Nations
role in coordinating relief effort, 101, 108

United Nations *(cont.)*
  role in implementation, 118, 122, 128, 129–31, 139. *See also* ONOMUZ
  standard operating procedures, 95
  team of observers, 103
United States
  interest in the peace process, 42–43, 47, 65
  official observer status, 80–83, 101
  pledge for humanitarian relief, 101
  support for the peace process, 56, 57, 62–65, 147
  technical advice, 74, 75, 84, 87, 95, 101

van Tonder, Maj. Gen. Cornelius, 20
Vatican diplomacy. *See* Holy See diplomacy

World Food Program, 108

ZANU, 7, 9–10
Zimbabwe
  independence, 10
  interests in Mozambique, 7, 13, 89, 97, 138
  ZANU sanctuaries in Mozambique, 7, 9–10
Zimbabwean African National Union. *See* ZANU
Zimbabwean troops in Mozambique, 19, 41, 43, 56, 58, 104, 115, 143, 144
Zuppi, Don Matteo
  leadership of Sant'Egidio group, 16, 18
  Nairobi meeting, 39, 41
  as observer/mediator at peace talks, 33, 37, 80, 81, 119, 122, 124, 130
  at peace accords ceremony, 3
  report on Round One, 35

United States Institute of Peace

The United States Institute of Peace is an independent, nonpartisan federal institution created and funded by Congress to strengthen the nation's capacity to promote the peaceful resolution of international conflict. Established in 1984, the Institute meets its congressional mandate through an array of programs, including grants, fellowships, conferences and workshops, library services, publications, and other educational activities. The Institute's Board of Directors is appointed by the President of the United States and confirmed by the Senate.

Board of Directors

ENDING MOZAMBIQUE'S WAR

The text of this book is set in Berkeley Oldstyle; the display type is Modern 735a. Cover design by Richard Lee Heffner; interior design by Day Wilkes Dosch and Joan Engelhardt; page makeup by Helene Y. Redmond of HYR Graphics.